D1155919

J.P. BICKELL

J.P. BICKELL

The Life, the Leafs, and the Legacy

Jason Wilson, Kevin Shea,
and Graham MacLachlan

DUNDURN
TORONTO

Printer: Friesens

Library and Archives Canada Cataloguing in Publication

Wilson, Jason, 1970-, author
       J.P. Bickell : the life, the Leafs, and the legacy / Jason Wilson, Kevin Shea, and Graham MacLachlan.

Includes bibliographical references and index.
Issued in print and electronic formats.
ISBN 978-1-4597-4046-4 (hardcover).--ISBN 978-1-4597-4047-1 (PDF).--ISBN 978-1-4597-4048-8 (EPUB)

       1. Bickell, J. P. 2. Hockey team owners--Canada--Biography.
3. Businessmen--Canada--Biography. 4. Toronto Maple Leafs (Hockey team)--Biography. 5. Toronto Maple Leafs (Hockey team)--History.
I. Shea, Kevin, 1956-, author II. MacLachlan, Graham, author III. Title.

GV848.5.B52W55 2017   796.962092   C2017-902801-4
                                                 C2017-902802-2

1 2 3 4 5   21 20 19 18 17

We acknowledge the support of the **Canada Council for the Arts**, which last year invested $153 million to bring the arts to Canadians throughout the country, and the **Ontario Arts Council** for our publishing program. We also acknowledge the financial support of the **Government of Ontario**, through the **Ontario Book Publishing Tax Credit** and the **Ontario Media Development Corporation**, and the **Government of Canada**.

Nous remercions le **Conseil des arts du Canada** de son soutien. L'an dernier, le Conseil a investi 153 millions de dollars pour mettre de l'art dans la vie des Canadiennes et des Canadiens de tout le pays.

Care has been taken to trace the ownership of copyright material used in this book. The author and the publisher welcome any information enabling them to rectify any references or credits in subsequent editions.
— *J. Kirk Howard, President*

The publisher is not responsible for websites or their content unless they are owned by the publisher.

Printed and bound in Canada.

VISIT US AT

 dundurn.com |  @dundurnpress | dundurnpress | dundurnpress

Dundurn
3 Church Street, Suite 500
Toronto, Ontario, Canada
M5E 1M2

The J.P. Bickell Foundation

Through the J.P. Bickell Foundation, John Paris Bickell has supported many Ontario charities and touched the lives of countless individuals. Established in 1953 through Mr. Bickell's Will, the philosophy of this registered charity has been shaped by its founder's belief in enriching society and serving the community. True to his wishes, the Foundation has supported a broad range of causes: from medicine to education, health and social welfare, and the arts.

The Foundation is the single largest donor for the Hospital for Sick Children in Toronto, providing a perpetual share of 50 percent of its income and supporting the hospital's research institute. At the time of Mr. Bickell's death, the hospital did not have an organized research institute; it now has Canada's leading pediatric health research institute and is recognized worldwide.

Following John Paris Bickell's death, the J.P. Bickell Foundation was established with a capital fund of approximately $13 million. Mr. Bickell provided his trustees, the National Trust Company, and now the Bank of Nova Scotia Trust Company (Scotiatrust®), with broad powers to distribute the balance of the Foundation's income as they saw fit. As of December 31, 2016, the capital market value of the Foundation has grown more than 1000 percent to a total of almost $144 million. Grants to charities have totalled almost $160 million.

The perpetual structure of the Foundation means that its support of numerous charities will continue for years to come. J.P. Bickell's legacy is one of extraordinary vision and generosity — a true pioneer in Canadian philanthropy.

Scotiatrust®, The Bank of Nova Scotia Trust Company
Trustee

Contents

Preface

My initial interest was not to write a book, but rather to find out more about the J.P. Bickell Memorial Award that I knew was associated with my first cousin, John Paris Bickell. We are a hockey family, and therefore this connection to the Toronto Maple Leafs sparked my interest. It is this that has led me to write about J.P. Bickell's life and legacy.

We always knew we were related to Mr. Bickell; however, we did not really understand the depth and breadth of his business interests or his contribution to the Canadian fabric, which we have since come to appreciate. During my research his name kept coming up. I always said, "It can't be the same guy!" … and invariably it was. Thankfully, I was able to locate a vast array of information, and to uncover those things that in many ways make up the cornerstone of what Canadians enjoy: in our health and wellness, our entertainment, our business environment, and our lifestyles. If you have benefited from medical research, been in a hospital, owned gold or silver, flown in an airplane, been in a movie theatre, or attended a professional sporting activity, you are most likely a beneficiary of J.P. Bickell. Through this book you will come to understand why.

The MacLachlan and Paris families were some of the first Scottish settlers in the Ottawa Valley in the mid-1800s and, more specifically, McNab Township. John Paris had the first grist mill: in the 1848 census he is listed as the only miller in the area. Of his twelve children, two of his daughters were named Agnes and Annie. Agnes was my great-grandmother and the older sister to Annie, who was J.P. Bickell's mother. Although the lives of the two sisters took different paths, they both lost their husbands prematurely.

Agnes (Paris) MacLachlan moved from White Lake, Ontario, with her eight children to settle her land claims northwest of Moose Jaw near Eyebrow, Saskatchewan, in 1905 — the year of that province's Confederation. It was her father, John Paris, who provided the wood from Ontario, some of the finest white oak there is, to build the family house and the barn that is one of the largest in western Canada.

This book, therefore, is a result of a family journey, and ultimately, of our quest for our families' legacy. It is our attempt to connect the dots of our ancestral past and to fill in and reconstruct part of our family tree for generations to come.

I have commissioned this book to honour J.P. Bickell, his parents Reverend David and Annie Bickell, and their children James Clark, John Paris, David Parkhurst, and Annie Gertrude (Marjorie). This endeavour will connect our families to the remarkable history that demonstrates, and celebrates, one man's life and legacy. His accomplishments are impressive. Overcoming the early loss of family members including his father, the family breadwinner, J.P. Bickell persevered and went on to achieve greatness, ultimately benefiting every Canadian along the way.

I dedicate this book to my immediate and extended family, past, present, and future. And to our readers, I hope this book will inspire you to research your own family legacy!

— Graham MacLachlan

Introduction

A Life in Full

J.P. Bickell was a dreamer. More, he was a dream-maker. Upon his death, the *Globe and Mail* prophesized that Bickell would one day have monuments erected to his memory

> from the Yukon to the financial districts of Toronto and Montreal. He will be remembered in London's Westminster, in New York and in Washington as a great executive, and in far places of the earth as an adventurer with a purpose.[1]

In actuality, little of this sort of commemoration ever came to pass. While he walked the earth Bickell lived an extraordinarily adventurous and purposeful life. His riches were, it must be said, wildly beyond most people's conception; so too was his benevolence. Given today's social media culture and thirst for news of the private lives of the rich and famous, it is unlikely that Bickell could have lived a life such as his now. A man of both his times and his means, Bickell was able to largely operate outside of the spotlight's direct glare. While his legacy, despite its considerable effects on an incalculable number of lives, has sadly remained shrouded. Frankly, given the breadth of his influence, the life of J.P. Bickell has been utterly under-celebrated. This is a historical disservice to a man who ranks as one of the most important builders of Toronto's institutional landscape and, indeed, the modern Canadian nation. Perhaps one of the main reasons his true import has been muted comes down to the character of the man himself. Bickell was always more comfortable orchestrating economic opuses and facilitating deeply improving social initiatives from well behind the scenes. Born in a church manse in Molesworth, Ontario, in 1884, John Paris Bickell would transcend his relatively modest beginnings to become one of Canada's true renaissance men of the first half of the twentieth century. JPB — or "Smiling Jack," as he was known to many — was fatherless at six, owned his own brokerage firm at twenty-three, and was a millionaire before he turned thirty. As one of the most important industrialists in Canadian history, J.P. Bickell cut an enormous swath across a nation that he helped to shape; kick-started several long-standing and successful businesses and organizations; transformed the city of Toronto; played a key role in the Allied cause during the Second World War; gave a leg-up to the diverse future careers of many in the business world; and ultimately exemplified the best of twentieth century philanthropy in Canada. Bickell made the lion's share of his riches on the city-side of mining, and was Ontario's first and likely most important producer of gold.[2] J.P.'s sage advice and assistance also gave form and funds to some of Canada's most famous, including, among others, Ontario Premier Mitchell Hepburn, Lord Beaverbrook, Jack Kent Cooke, Roy Thomson, Nathan L. Nathanson, Sydney Logan, and, perhaps most famously, of course, Conn Smythe. Yet Bickell's work touched far more not-so-famous people. As a board member of Wellesley Hospital, Bickell was intimately involved in several philanthropic endeavours throughout his life; and his eponymous foundation, to which he left most of his millions, has advanced several streams of medical research and care in Canada.

Certainly, Bickell was not flawless. He drank to excess, gambled with caprice, was inclined to keep company that was perhaps a little too "interesting," and went on far too many and sometimes unnecessary escapades. As a man who loved risk, Bickell went on to court several close calls during his life, most of these the result of his audacious lust for adventure. In many ways, his several near-death experiences only added to the mythology of the man.[3]

This mythology grew exponentially over the course of Bickell's life, a life large enough to include many different Bickells: there was Bickell the broker; Bickell the banker; Bickell the builder; Bickell the "Busy B"; Bickell the bomber; and, perhaps most outstandingly, Bickell the benevolent. All along, J.P. rarely refused himself any of the grandest and often ostentatious treasures that a millionaire of his day could acquire. Doubtless, this penchant for the grandiose more often than not ended up serving the greater good. Anne Logan, author and daughter of Sydney H. Logan, president of the Canadian Bank of Commerce and one of Bickell's closest friends, attested that J.P. was "flamboyant but through this trait he contributed much to the happiness of others."[4]

At the age of thirty-six Bickell retired from the brokerage firm that he himself had established and in which he made his first million. He resolved to concentrate all of his formidable energies on mining gold. As president of McIntyre Porcupine Mines Limited, Bickell soon graduated to multi-millionaire status and contributed greatly to the communities of Schumacher, Porcupine, and Timmins. By 1955, only four years after Bickell's death, the company had produced $230 million worth of gold, had paid its shareholders over $62 million in dividends, and had employed hundreds of families in the greater Timmins area.

J.P. fit the early twentieth century Canadian cliché of rich-mining-magnate-*cum*-hockey-man. Not unlike others in the mining industry, he chose to include hockey within his portfolio; he was part owner of the Toronto St. Patricks before that team underwent a shocking and historic metamorphosis. Spurred on by Conn Smythe, one of hockey's all-time characters, Bickell helped lead the franchise to become one of the most storied teams in professional sport: the Toronto Maple Leafs.

In the grand narrative of the Maple Leafs, however, the role of Conn Smythe has been slightly exaggerated while Bickell's has been somewhat soft-pedalled. The two friends, nevertheless, worked together to form a team that manufactured astounding results, both on and off the ice. Perhaps most impressively, the company they created built one of the hockey world's finest coliseums: Maple Leaf Gardens. They managed this remarkable achievement during the misery of the Great Depression. In essence, Bickell, as he would do for so many others, facilitated Smythe's dream of an ice palace for Toronto's winter warriors.

The dream-maker was involved in a head-spinning number of diverse interests and institutions. Bickell was an appointed director of the Canadian Bank of Commerce (now CIBC), Art Gallery of Toronto (now the Art Gallery of Ontario), National Trust Company (now Scotiabank), International Nickel Company of Canada (INCO), and, perhaps most famously, Maple Leaf Gardens, of which he was the first president. He also had his hand in the movie business and helped Nathanson put together the links of his Famous Players chain. Importantly, Bickell was a senior partner in the notable New York stock brokerage Thomson and McKinnon. And the list goes on. By the end of the 1930s, there was scarcely an industry in Ontario that J.P. Bickell did not have a hand *in* or understanding *of*.

Politically, Bickell was tight with Ontario's Depression-era Liberal premier Mitchell Hepburn. It was an association that was not without its trials and, by virtue of the premier's volatility and antagonistic relationship with Prime Minister Mackenzie King, it sometimes put Bickell in a political pickle. "Mitch" and "Smiling Jack" were close, nevertheless, and worked together to build a fully functional economic machine for the province, while establishing a veritable rat-pack of private associates and buddies. This assemblage of politicians, captains of industry, and stockbrokers virtually annexed Toronto's King Edward Hotel: the King Eddy served as both bastion for the Liberal Party and rumpus-room for the bacchanal behaviour of what can only be described as an old boys' club, Hepburn and Bickell being two of the main boys.

Though Bickell loved his life in the fast lane (he juggled three girlfriends, all of whom were nurses he had met at Wellesley Hospital), his patriotic duty was inviolate. When war broke out in 1939, Bickell went to England and joined a four-some that would be known as the Four Busy B's. This group, led by Lord Beaverbrook, included former Canadian prime minister R.B. Bennett, Toronto-born British MP Beverley Baxter, and Bickell. At first, Bickell was in charge of moving aircraft from the factories to the airfields for both training and operational procedures. It was a job that was vital to stopping Hitler's plans to invade the United Kingdom during the famous Battle of Britain.

Following this successful chapter of his war, Bickell returned to Canada as president of Malton Ontario's Victory Aircraft. Victory held the crucial responsibility of constructing and delivering Lancaster bombers to the Allies. The "Lanc" was known as the shining sword of the RAF's Bomber Command. Despite all of his numerous and noteworthy pre-war appointments, Bickell's wartime roles were no doubt his most important.

Bickell kept up his impossible pace after the war. He helped fund and establish aircraft manufacturer A.V. Roe Canada, publicly rallied against Canada's coming off of the gold standard, and set about crafting a legacy that would, upon his passing, see some $13 million donated to charity. This money established the J.P. Bickell Foundation which, since its inception, has paid out over $160 million to charity, including more than $76 million to the Hospital for Sick Children.

Alas, ours is an imperfect biography. While it is easy to track the trajectory of Bickell's business and philanthropic endeavours, it is far more difficult to fully seize the man's true essence. The *Toronto Telegram* described Bickell as a "stocky man with iron grey hair, a hearty laugh and a weakness for cigars."[5] But — does this touch on his *essence*? As there was no trove of memoirs or cache of personal letters available, we are left guessing as to what drove the man to leave such a healthy and, for its time, matchless nest egg to charity. Did the loss of his father and two young brothers light a fire in the belly of a man who would personally bankroll such vital medical research during his life and afterward? We are likewise left guessing as to his personal affairs. Though "Smiling Jack" had many lady friends and was regarded by many as the richest bachelor in Canada, he never married. Was there a custodian of his heart who has been lost to the passage of time? While we may never know the answer to these questions, we can be certain that, apart from being one of the most successful Canadians of his generation, J.P. Bickell added richly to the lives of so very many people, most of whom he would never meet.[6] We may not be able to penetrate the emotions of this champion of the mining industry, but we can bear testament to his munificence. The Foundation that bears his name has pledged to ensure that "his deeds will not pass away, nor his name wither."[7] It is hoped that this work will — at least in some small measure — be their safeguard.

John Paris Bickell.

1

Gold

From a Manse in Molesworth

John Paris Bickell was named after his grandfather John Paris, born in 1808 in Stow, Roxburghshire, in the Scottish Borderlands. Historically, the area had seen some of the heaviest of the fighting and suffered the worst of the constant raiding during Scotland's Wars of Independence, a series of conflicts that spanned the late twelfth through fifteenth centuries.[1] Many more years passed before the land knew lasting peace. By the nineteenth century, however, the Borders, and Stow in particular, had become an important hub for the wool and agricultural industries. It was from here that John Paris immigrated to Canada in the 1840s.

Paris settled with his wife Isabella in Renfrew County, west of Ottawa. During this time Upper Canada was rebounding from an economic downturn, as Britain moved to freer trade and dissolution of the mercantile system that favoured colonial trade. This put pressure on various industries, but farmers were not hit nearly as hard as merchants.[2] Indeed, there was generally a strong economic recovery during the decade the Paris family arrived in

The manse in Molesworth, Ontario, where J.P. Bickell was born in 1884.

the Province of Canada. As a result, the Paris family thrived in Renfrew. Isabella gave birth to their eighth child, Annie, J.P.'s mother, in 1857.

J.P.'s other grandfather had migrated from Plymouth, England, in 1832, settling in Dundas, Ontario. His son David Bickell, who became J.P.'s father, was born and bred in Beverly Township in Halton County, Ontario. David, who was a farmer, married Annie Paris on November 8, 1882.

David Bickell gave up his profession to become a Presbyterian minister. He was soon given a small charge in Mount Forest, Ontario, where Annie took a job as a schoolteacher. David and Annie produced four children: James Clark, born in May 1883; John Paris, born in September 1884; David Parkhurst, born in August 1888 (he died at the tender age of four); and Annie Gertrude, better known as Marjorie, who was born in November 1890.[3]

J.P. was born in the family manse in Molesworth, Ontario, on September 26, 1884. He was still a boy when his father died on February 3, 1891, of enteritis (inflammation of the intestines) and peritonitis (inflammation of the abdomen).[4] David Bickell, Sr. was only thirty-five years old when he left his wife Annie and his children, eight-year-old James, six-year-old J.P., two-year-old David Jr., and three-month-old Marjorie. The *Huron Expositor* proclaimed:

> The death is announced of Rev. David Bickell of Mount Forest, after a short illness from inflammation of the bowels. Mr. Bickell had been in the ministry for the past eight years, and was a promising young divine of the Presbyterian Church. He leaves a wife and four children.[5]

The good reverend's passing came while J.P. was just starting his schooling.

The young J.P. saw a fair amount of death in his early life. While it can only be speculation, this no doubt contributed to his later intense interest and investments in medical care and research. Only two years after mourning the death of his father, J.P. lost his younger brother David Jr. in 1893. The eight-year-old J.P. had now lost two members of his smallish (for the times) family. In 1896 Annie moved the family to Calgary, Alberta, for the health of the children, yet more heartache beckoned as J.P. then lost his older brother James Clark in 1898 from appendicitis when James was only fourteen. Now only thirteen years of age, with only his mother Annie and baby sister Marjorie remaining, J.P. found himself as the man of the house. Immediately upon James's death, Annie moved the family back to Toronto in June 1898. J.P. was now forced to contemplate the real world a little ahead of schedule. In order to support his family he found work, first in a candy store and later as a junior clerk in a meat-packing plant.[6] Bickell was actually fired from the clerk position due to his "extramural moneymaking activities."[7] This graft, however,

Reverend David Bickell, photographed in Molesworth Presbyterian Church, 1885.

allowed Bickell to stay on at St. Andrew's College, where he was among the first hundred boys enrolled, until he was eighteen. Jack, as he became known to his closest friends at St. Andrew's, had an entrepreneurial spirit that was not confined to odd jobs in Toronto. The boy was determined to raise the necessary funds to finish his education wherever he could, and that even included work within the hallowed walls of St. Andrew's itself.

Bickell's academic career, especially taken in consideration with the achievements he managed in his life, was *not* conspicuous. A registration card from his time at the college confirmed that Bickell "knew little of how to be a student — supported himself while at school by selling tea, a good lad — was a boarder for one term."[8] One collegiate contemporary wrote of the young man: "I beheld J.P. Bickell auctioning off goods at a great rate. By appearance he was having a lot to say for himself and for his goods too."[9] The salesman managed to achieve his aim and graduated from St. Andrew's as part of the Class of 1902.[10]

Annie Christina Bickell (née Paris), born in McNab Township in Renfrew, Ontario.

Even as a youth, Bickell's exaggerated sense of adventure was apparent. A trip to Dawson City during the Klondike may have spurred an interest in precious metals.[11] (Bickell would famously return to Dawson with his twin-engine plane in what was a near-catastrophic trip in the late 1930s.) Bickell's first *real* training in terms of the world of finance, however, took place not in the tweedy environs of St. Andrew's, but rather on the busy floors of the grain exchange in Chicago. While there, Bickell learned all that he could about the grain exchange. Presciently, he began to establish a network of highly influential friends and associates in the Windy City that would help the St. Andrew's grad at various junctures in his business life.[12]

J.P.'s mother Annie and his sister Marjorie were also living in Toronto.[13] As of 1906, J.P.'s official Toronto address was the same as his mother's, presumably so he could have a convenient place to stay on his trips back and forth from Chicago. At this time, Bickell was holding down a position as secretary-treasurer for the confectioners McGregor-Harris Company, and all the while plotting his future.

J.P. Bickell's sister Marjorie.

Bickell the Broker

In 1907 Bickell took his first huge step toward financial reward when he established J.P. Bickell & Co. This financial brokerage business was located at 15–19 King Street West in the Standard Bank Building at the corner of King and Jordan Streets, just steps west of Yonge Street in Toronto. Bickell rented space on the top floor, the eighth. He was only twenty-three.[14]

In his new venture, Bickell was an American agent after a fashion, trading on behalf of some very heavy U.S. speculators that he had met while in Chicago. Bickell was fortunate to have entered the brokerage game at just the right time: Canada, and in Ontario in particular, was experiencing a significant mining boom, and Toronto swiftly became the storefront for Canada's mining industry. While this would position Bickell nicely for his biggest windfall, it was grain that brought Bickell's quick and early success.

To be sure, J.P. knew grain. As he was tied in with some of the more important American grain speculators, Bickell was head and shoulders above other Toronto brokers who were new to the emerging grain game.[15] Bickell was soon well established on the broker side of the industry. According to the Toronto City Directory of 1913, J.P. Bickell & Co. Brokers were members of the Chicago Board of Trade, the Winnipeg Grain Exchange, the New York Produce Exchange, and the Toronto Standard Stock and Mining Exchange, and were "correspondents" for Finley, Barrell & Co. who were (the advertisement trumpeted) "members of all leading exchanges."[16] Wherever it mattered, J.P. shrewdly found comprehensive representation. As an agent for his friends back in Chicago, Bickell was trading as much as four million bushels a day. Indeed, Bickell was making bushels of money himself. For his efforts on behalf of only one of his American associates, for example, J.P. received a $250,000 commission.[17]

With each win, Bickell's sphere of influence expanded exponentially. His small circle of associates was one that had to be reckoned with. Frederick J. Crawford, for instance, was one of Bickell's associates before branching out on his own. Crawford would also become a director of the Toronto Maple Leaf Hockey Club, and he later replaced Nathan L. Nathanson — yet another Bickell associate — as the CBC governor in 1943.[18] Part of Bickell's genius was the ability to connect the dots and people in his life, drawing on his ever-growing resources and bridging his various connections on both sides of the border. He was therefore able to call upon many disparate interests to serve his purposes. While this made Bickell a very wealthy man, it also profoundly influenced an untold number of souls whose lives were positively affected by the man's successes.

Bickell was willing to share his knowledge with anyone who showed initiative. This included teaching at Frontier College. Founded by Alfred Fitzpatrick in 1899, the college was an experiment that anticipated post–Second World War initiatives to provide ordinary working people with access to higher learning.

The college was an expression of the social gospel movement; social gospellers fused tenets of self-improvement and intellectual betterment with traditional Protestant principles of sobriety, moral probity and, importantly, work ethic.[19] Ignorance was, according to Fitzpatrick, "the worker's enslavement."[20] To liberate the lumberman, the navvy, and the miner from ignorance, Fitzpatrick enlisted several "labourer-teachers," educated men who were successful and hard-working. Hundreds of these university men came to the college to instruct the working students. Among the more famous labourer-teachers were Norman Bethune, James R. Mutchmore, Albert E. Ottewell, and J.P. Bickell, who never forgot his time there.[21]

The brokerage business, however, did not always prove to be smooth sailing. Bickell's office had its fair share of legal contests, perhaps not surprising given the vast sums that were travelling back and forth across the wire and, importantly, across the border. It was often the brokers' practice to ignore the ever-fluctuating exchange rates between Canada and the United States. This obviously set up disagreements in regard to who was liable for the exchange rate difference, and sometimes the cases were escalated to the Supreme Court of Canada.[22] Regardless of any setbacks he may have had, connected as he was to the Chicago Board of Trade, the Chicago and Winnipeg grain exchanges, and the New York produce and cotton exchanges, Bickell's office handled one of the largest grain trading businesses in North America.[23]

Yet even the extraordinary success of his brokerage was not enough for Bickell. In late 1919 he announced that he would be retiring from the brokerage firm that he had raised to concentrate on his many other interests, specifically mining.

Control of the brokerage moved to A.L. Hudson & Co., which had been connected with the Bickell firm for several years.

As the *Toronto Star* reported:

> Mr. Bickell will devote his entire time to his various mining interests which have, in fact, received the greater part of his attention for some years past. As chief executive of the Temiskaming and McIntyre Mines, he already has a large and increasing responsibility, and, in addition, has interests in other mining properties on both sides of the border.[24]

At thirty-six, he had more than proven his worth on the floors of the various stock exchanges. He now turned his energy to proving his worth in gold.

Yellow Metal

The would-be millionaire had first become interested in the metals of the earth during a trip to the Yukon goldfields as a young man. Then, in 1903, the Cobalt silver strike near Lake Temiskaming signalled the beginning of Ontario's own mineral "Klondike." The find attracted many optimistic prospectors to stake their claims; along with their dreams, they rode north on the railroads that were being built to link these remote areas to the south. Toronto, with its stock exchange, would become the storefront for the precious metals mining trade.

After the Cobalt strike, J.P. secured seats on the Standard Stock and Mining Exchange. Like so many others he continued to keep a sharp eye on Cobalt, and soon he went into business with mining mogul Burr Cartwright. Their relationship was further galvanized when things started to heat up in the Temiskaming area. The mine Cartwright oversaw was prosperous, and Bickell benefited from this relationship by helping Cartwright develop his silver mine. Bickell became even further invested in mining in 1906, when William G. Trethewey sold his eponymous silver mine for $1 million to a group that included Bickell and the English investor Colonel Alexander Hay.[25]

Yet it was gold that had the widest appeal. The Porcupine Gold Rush of 1909 profoundly affected not only Ontario's hinterland and the small towns north of Sudbury, but also the entire province. The development of its mining industry and the investments in mining paid dividends for Ontario and its residents, and contributed to an overall higher standard of living.[26]

Bickell was still young. Having developed the silver mine at Cobalt, and with that trip to the Yukon goldfields still haunting his imagination, he now set his sights on the yellow metal of Timmins. The McIntyre Porcupine gold mine was one of the most important gold strikes in Canadian history. Three mines

— Hollinger, Dome, and McIntyre — were discovered by separate prospectors within a few miles of each other and were at the heart of the gold rush. The Big Three, which would subsequently control 90 percent of the region's gold production, collectively produced over 67 million ounces of gold during the twentieth century, and were responsible for the establishment of the city of Timmins, Ontario.[27]

The region's early stakes had been courtesy of the Scotsman Sandy McIntyre (a.k.a. Alexander Oliphant), who had left Glasgow for Canada in 1903. McIntyre would soon become central to the J.P. Bickell story. Along with a German-born prospector named Hans Buttner, McIntyre travelled the shores of Pearl Lake in search of gold. In 1909, on the very same day that the Hollinger team made its discovery, McIntyre and Buttner found visible gold. The pair subsequently staked claims and went about developing what would become the McIntyre mine, which would forever change this entire region of Ontario.

Sandy McIntyre and Hans Buttner staking the McIntyre mine claim.

Sandy McIntyre, discoverer of the McIntyre mine in Schumacher, Ontario, October 23, 1909.

The man known in Glasgow as Alexander Oliphant had unceremoniously left his wife back in Scotland before sailing to Canada under his new name, McIntyre. It was no secret that Sandy was overly fond of alcohol, a common trait among the prospectors of his era. Living up to the cliché, however, cost him dearly. Indeed, McIntyre must have been thoroughly sloshed when he sold off his stakes in the Porcupine for such laughably low fees. He sold a quarter-interest, for instance, to Weldon Young of Ottawa for a paltry $300. That same day he sold an eighth-interest to Jim Hughes for a mere $25. Later, he sold a half-interest to A.J. Young of North Bay for $5,000. There was a $60,000 option included in that deal, but McIntyre was apparently tricked out of it. In the end, McIntyre had sold his 1909 stakes for a pittance when one considers the millions that would one day be mined out of the Porcupine. In what can only be regarded as a compassionate move, McIntyre Porcupine Gold Mines Limited gave Sandy a pension to see him through his later years.[28]

A New York group that included Charles Flynn and his family, and stockbroker Albert Freeman, had been assembling the loose strings of Sandy McIntyre's initial stakes with mixed results. The group had managed to accumulate some eighty thousand shares, including a large purchase from then New York Governor Nathan Miller.[29] For his part, Bickell became entrenched in the Porcupine mines in 1911 when Flynn's New York group was effectively on its way out. Alec Gillies, who was a client of Bickell's brokerage, was the one who truly got J.P. interested in McIntyre Porcupine. As Clary Dixon, a prospector who had staked claims in the Porcupine area, recounted, "Alec persuaded him to buy the Pearl Lake water claims."[30] The eventual result was that Sandy McIntyre's original claims would make up only a small portion of the total acreage.

The accumulation of property did not, however, happen overnight. Perhaps waiting for the gold dust to settle after that initial 1909 rush, Bickell bought and also sold.

In March 1911 McIntyre Porcupine Mines Limited was incorporated with an initial capital of $1 million.[31] The original holdings included 145 acres on both sides of Pearl Lake. An additional 34 acres were acquired from West McIntyre, as were an additional 68 acres underlying Pearl Lake. Bickell wanted to acquire the claims under Pearl Lake that were jointly held by Gillies and Governor Miller. Gillies and Miller and their new partner Percy Parker soon optioned their claims to Bickell for $100,000. Bickell then quickly flipped his newly acquired land running along the McIntyre property. As mining historian Philip Smith explains, Bickell agreed to a package deal through Freeman, who negotiated on Bickell's behalf:

> $100,000, which was what the claims had cost him, plus the $4,000 he had spent in work on them, plus — and one senses he considered this far more important — a piece of the action, in the shape of seventy thousand McIntyre shares.[32]

"Smiling Jack" was planning for the future.

Fortuitously, Bickell acquired another vital piece of the puzzle via the New York group he soon would be succeeding. At their request, R.J. "Dick" Ennis was brought from Colorado to Porcupine in 1911. Ennis really kept the mine going and was put in charge of McIntyre's mining and milling operations. Under Ennis, the mine was the first in the country to use rubber liners in milling, the first to sink a shaft below four thousand feet, and the first to employ a full-time metallurgist on the mill staff. Ennis held this position for forty years, retiring only a few months before his death in 1951. In Ennis, Bickell (who died that same year) was gifted one of the most resourceful hands in the world of mining. Richard Joseph Ennis was inducted into the Canadian Mining Hall of Fame in 2003.

The Bickell-Ennis tandem would write mining history in Canada — that is, after a long, precarious prelude. To be sure, the assays were sparse to begin with and development was weighed down with a host of difficulties. Bankruptcy loomed at several junctures.[33] And Bickell was still somewhat handcuffed by the board that had the marks of the New York group imprinted all over it. The determined Bickell-Ennis team was not put off, however. Bickell, as Clary Dixon observed, was willing to learn from Ennis's mining acumen: "Bickell always listened to Dick Ennis, and Dick knew his stuff."[34]

Trusting in his manager's multifarious skill sets, Bickell busied himself with the business of buying up the other parts of Pearl Lake. The accumulation of property did not immediately translate into success, as Dixon confessed:

> The early days were something, a regular circus. The first stock was sold in the States, you know, at about $2 a share. Damned company was reorganized and stockholders cut down 80 per cent. It was a case of tough titty and no teeth. Company always in debt.[35]

In the end, it was ingenuity, gumption, and guile that kept the company going.

The McIntyre mine as it appeared in the 1920s.

In what might very well be a case of romance lusting after fact, Ennis is said to have averted a crisis by rushing a still-hot gold brick to the bank to meet the company's payroll and to save the friendly bank manager embarrassment after he'd put his neck on the line for Ennis and company.[36] Dixon also recalled how Ennis would "hide underground whenever creditors came to the mine howling about unpaid bills."[37] When the miners went out on strike in 1913, the writing appeared to be on the wall for McIntyre Porcupine. The company tried to sell stock to Hollinger at a paltry thirty-five cents, but even this price was considered too high. These were despairing times.

Bickell, as director, came to the rescue.

Essentially, Bickell kept McIntyre Porcupine afloat on his own dime. In 1913 Bickell put out a $250,000 bond issue to finance a three-hundred-ton mill. Yet, even with a promised bonus of one thousand free shares with every $1,000 bond, no one seemed interested in investing. Bickell and Ennis were, however, able to persuade some of the machinery companies into taking bonds for equipment. Likewise, Ennis was also able to persuade the mine's doctor to take 550 shares in the

R.J. "Dick" Ennis, general manager of McIntyre Mines.

company in lieu of his cash fee. Dixon aptly described the company's anxious situation: "McIntyre was the biggest joke in Porcupine."[38] But it was no joke for Bickell, who remained resolute. J.P. loaned the company money to meet the most pressing bills while personally guaranteeing notes to others. This included wages and taxes.[39]

Bickell had been elected a director when Freeman, the man who had once negotiated on Bickell's behalf, resigned. It was no secret that J.P. did not appreciate how Freeman had been doing business. Inexplicably, at least as far as Bickell was concerned, Freeman, who was then out on bail, was reinstated as president of McIntyre by the board in April 1914.[40] As historian Philip Smith surmised:

> Bickell was certainly even more displeased a few months later when a board meeting at which he was not present agreed to redeem, or buy back, Freeman's holding of McIntyre Porcupine bonds. Freeman agreed to part with the bonds at thirty per cent below their face value, but the board's action was clearly illegal: the holders of a company's bonds have first claim on its assets, and Freeman had no right to get his money out before all the other bond-holders could be paid off.[41]

This may have been the straw that broke the camel's back. Bickell was determined now to take charge of McIntyre Porcupine and to squeeze Freeman and his crew out of the scene altogether. On May 5, 1915, Freeman stepped aside, explaining to the shareholders that the company no longer needed his services. That same day, Colonel Alexander M. Hay replaced Freeman as president, and Sir Henry Pellatt (of Casa Loma fame) was named vice-president.[42] From this point forward, it was effectively Bickell who built the company into one of the greatest mining companies in Canada and the world.[43]

In 1915, the McIntyre Extension Company was formed. An additional 120 acres were acquired from the Pearl Lake Company. At the same time, the McIntyre Jupiter Company took over the holdings of the Jupiter mine. In 1916, the three companies, McIntyre Porcupine, McIntyre Extension, and McIntyre Jupiter, were amalgamated under Colonel Hay's presidency. Hay, along with W.J. Sheppard and J.B. Tudhope, were all prominent mining men brought in by Bickell to bring together the disparate pieces around Pearl Lake. The Colonel served as McIntyre Porcupine's president from April 1915 until January 1917. He died only one day before McIntyre declared its first dividend.[44]

More happily, the mine's shaft began to tap into the more favourable greenstone area. The ore, albeit slowly, began to improve. And as the grades of gold improved, the McIntyre Porcupine, thanks to Bickell's stewardship, had successfully negotiated those early turbulent waters.

Ennis too, was crucial to the company's survival, and was rightly credited with the rapid development of the mine below the so-called five-hundred-foot horizon (the point when a mine becomes a going concern).[45] Indeed, by 1916 all liabilities had been discharged, and the first dividend was ready to be paid out in 1917.[46] McIntyre Porcupine could now count itself within Porcupine's "Big Three." Bickell had seen the bleakest days of the company through and would remain as chairman of the board until his death.

When McIntyre Porcupine began to stabilize during the First World War, Bickell began to explore other mining prospects. In 1916 Bickell was the treasurer of Adanac Silver Mines, working the silver deposits in Cobalt, Ontario. He was also the president of the Superstition Mining Company of Arizona.[47] A decade on, Bickell was effectively overseeing several other mining interests including Capitol Silver Mines. Yet it was J.P.'s main company that continued to flower. By 1917 Bickell was now officially the president of McIntyre Porcupine, as the *Porcupine Advance* reported:

> At a meeting of the directors of the McIntyre Porcupine Mines Co. last week Mr. J.P. Bickell, broker, Toronto, who has been connected with the Company from its early days, and has been a member of the board of directors since 1913, was chosen as President to succeed the late Col. A.M. Hay. Mr. Bickell's experience and interest with the Company during the days of its growth should make him a capable head, as he will undoubtedly be an earnest one, in the coming days of further progress and development of the McIntyre Mines.[48]

It was an apt prophecy. Further progress continued with accelerating speed under Bickell's presidency.

The McIntyre mine itself was only 64 acres when Bickell came aboard. Under Bickell's stewardship, the area was extended to 1,436 acres.[49] McIntyre Porcupine also had taken over the Belleterre gold mine in Quebec as well as the Castle-Trethewey silver mine near Gowganda, Ontario. Bickell had been the president of Castle-Trethewey in 1923 and 1924. At the end of 1935, Bickell, acting on behalf of Castle-Trethewey (as it was a subsidiary of McIntyre Porcupine) undertook to organize and finance a new company: Omega Gold Mines Limited, working out of Kirkland Lake. The Platt Vet mine, which at first seemed hopeless, also began to produce encouraging results. A group consisting of D.M. Hogarth, Charles Kaeding, Bernard E. Smith, and Bickell was also invested to the tune of $500,000 in the Madsen mine at Red Lake.[50] Yet, while these other investments proved fruitful, albeit in varying degrees, it was the McIntyre Porcupine mine that remained the bedrock of Bickell's great fortune.[51]

According the Ontario Department of Mines *Annual Report* in 1936, McIntyre Porcupine Mines Limited, with Bickell as president and his good American friend "Sell 'Em Ben" Smith installed as vice-president, was remarkably successful. Employing over 1,200 people, the company had an authorized capitalization of 800,000 shares of $5 per value. Of these, some 798,000 had been issued.[52] The McIntyre also yielded handsome returns for its shareholders; it remains one of the most important mines in Canadian history. Between 1912 and 1955 the total production was valued at $230 million. By the time of Bickell's death, the company had already paid its shareholders over $62 million in dividends, and had employed hundreds of families in the Timmins area.[53] By 1976, when the company changed ownership, the McIntyre Porcupine Mine had produced 10.6 million ounces of gold, valued at $367.5 million.[54]

J.P. Bickell holding five gold bars while the McIntyre mine's directors look on.

The Inner Circle

By the time Bickell had taken control of McIntyre Porcupine, he was already considering different endeavours. In addition to the import of his brokerage days and his crucial role in Canada's precious metal industry, these extended his stunningly wide reach into many different social, political, economic, and even cultural domains. To assist him in these endeavours, J.P. assembled a diverse cast of characters that would serve as his own personal micro-ministry.

Such was the rags-to-riches story of "Sell 'Em Ben" Smith, Bickell's closest friend, that Smith could have been the protagonist in a Horatio Alger novel. Smith, whose parents had come to America from Ireland, had been a fight promoter before starting out as a $9-per-week Wall Street clerk.[55] He then reputedly turned a borrowed $100 into $35,000 when he was only fifteen. A field ambulance driver with the American Ambulance Service during the first two years of the First World War, Smith also figured in the mythology surrounding New York's Automobile Row, famously choosing to take a 5 percent commission over a fixed salary when he was a car salesman.[56] He developed a reputation for buying in and out of stocks during some of the most vulnerable days of the Depression-era market.

Smith made his money through equal measures of caprice and acumen. In fact, he made somewhere in the region of $10 million on the "bear" side, short-selling stocks during the month of the 1929 stock market crash.[57] Smith was regarded by many, including the *Saturday Evening Post*, to be "the legendary biggest bear in Wall Street history."[58] The so-called short sellers were accused of being unpatriotic and of acerbating and prolonging the Depression. U.S. President Herbert Hoover, for instance, identified Smith as the principal trader responsible for the economic decline, particularly in 1932. For his part, Smith made no apologies for his short-selling days, though he was displeased with the negative attention and subsequent investigation that came his way. When Hoover's time was up, however, Ben was welcomed back into the political fold. In part due to his admiration and financial support for Roosevelt and his tide-shifting New Deal campaign, Smith turned from bear to bull and was remarkably part of the president's entourage on the day of his inauguration.[59]

Smith took a shine to certain individuals and, like his Canadian friend J.P., became their angel and dream facilitator. He helped Garfield Weston, for one, to break his family's business into the British baking market.[60] Smith's oft-quoted catch-phrase was: "Sell 'em, they're not worth anything."[61] This bear-*cum*-bull was a member of Bickell's inner sanctum, and perhaps, more than any other, had the ear of his millionaire friend.

So, too, at least for a time, did Nathan L. Nathanson, who was installed as a director of Maple Leaf Gardens at Bickell's prompting. Long before then, Bickell had served as vice-president of Nathanson's then-fledgling movie company, Famous Players.[62] Yet Bickell's involvement in the movie industry preceded his days with Nathanson's Famous Players Canadian Corporation. J.P. had previously served as president of both Eastern Theatres Limited

Bernard E. "Sell 'Em Ben" Smith, Bickell's friend and director of McIntyre Mines.

and Hamilton United Theatres Limited.[63] Eastern Theatres, for example, oversaw the construction of Toronto's Pantages Theatre, which specialized in the era's wildly popular vaudeville acts.[64] Similarly, Bickell also served as vice-president of the Select Pictures Corporation's Canadian distribution company.[65] Bickell was also part of the team that acquired Montreal's Théâtre St-Denis in October 1917.[66]

Importantly, Bickell was vice-president of the Regent Theatre Company. The Regent Theatre was one of Toronto's first large movie theatres and stood on Adelaide between Yonge and Bay Streets.[67] The theatre's company was formed in 1916 by a group of Toronto financiers that included P.W. Cushman, E.L. Ruddy, W.J. Sheppard, J.B. Tudhope and, of course, Bickell. Anticipating the ever-increasing interest in moving pictures, the company sought to acquire and transform J. Ambrose Small's theatre, The Majestic, into a deluxe movie theatre, truly the first of its kind in Canada.[68]

The Regent was magnificent. The theatre offered moviegoers world-class entertainment that included first-run Paramount films, a playbill that was changed thrice weekly, and (as advertised) "competitive" admission fees.[69] The Regent Theatre Company also had an eleven-thousand-dollar Casavant concert organ installed. The company then hired top-tier musicians to provide music to accompany the silent films. The formal opening of the Regent came in the middle of the First World War on Saturday, August 26, 1916, when *Little Lady Eileen* starring Marguerite Clark was screened.[70]

Meanwhile, Nathanson had his eyes set on a national circuit of theatres. By 1919 he was operating a total of sixteen movie theatres across Canada. In January 1920 the Nathanson group sought to take their movie business to the next level and formed the Famous Players Canadian Corporation. In fact, Famous Players, which had a formal partnership with the American company Paramount Theatres Ltd., was founded by Nathanson in Bickell's office.[71] J.P.'s friend W.D. Ross, head of the Bank of Nova Scotia and later Lieutenant-Governor of Ontario, I.W. Killam of Royal Securities, Sir Herbert Holt of the Royal Bank, and Bickell were all members of the board of directors that underwrote the necessary $4 million of the company's initial share offerings.[72] The vision for Famous Players was to own fifty theatres across the country and become the number one movie theatre chain in Canada. It was a vision that sent shockwaves around the silver screen world, as the *New York Clipper* attested on January 28, 1920:

> The new company, which will be a purely Canadian company, will own seven theatres in Toronto, six of which are already in operation. It will also take over twenty theatres which are already operating in various parts of the country, and it is expected that in a little over a year the new houses to complete the coast-to-coast chain will be completed, with a total seating capacity of 45,000. Places in Ontario, other than Toronto, at which the company will operate: Guelph, Galt, Kingston, Port Hope and Hamilton. The money involved in the establishment in the new chain of theatres is placed at between ten and fifteen million dollars. Mr. J.P. Bickell, of Toronto and J.B. Tudhope, MP, of Orillia, are among the directors, and it is rumoured that Lord Beaverbrook will also have a financial interest in it.[73]

By 1921 Famous Players was well on its way, owning twenty-nine theatres and reporting earnings of $291,987.91. The following year, the company earned $380,839.97.

Despite its obvious association with the American Paramount company, Famous Players appealed to many Canadians because of

Famous Players
Canadian Corporation
LIMITED

EIGHT ANNUAL
REPORT AND
CONSOLIDATED
BALANCE SHEET

August 27th, 1927

Famous Players Canadian Corporation 1927 Annual Report.

OFFICERS

ADOLPH ZUKOR...*President*
J. P. BICKELL...*Vice-President*
N. L. NATHANSON.....................................*Managing Director*
ARTHUR COHEN...*Secretary-Treasurer*
THOS. J. BRAGG...*Comptroller*

———

FINANCE COMMITTEE

J. P. BICKELL   S. R. KENT
HONOURABLE WILLIAM D. ROSS, *Chairman*

———

DIRECTORS

J. P. BICKELL, President, McIntyre Porcupine Mines, Ltd.
SIR HERBERT HOLT, President, Royal Bank of Canada.
S. R. KENT, Paramount Famous Lasky Corporation., N.Y.
I. W. KILLAM, President, Royal Securities Corp., Limited.
N. L. NATHANSON, Managing Director.
HON. WILLIAM D. ROSS, Director, Bank of Nova Scotia.
W. J. SHEPPARD, Director, Royal Bank of Canada.
J. B. TUDHOPE, President, Carriage Factories, Ltd.
SIR WILLIAM WISEMAN, New York City.
ADOLPH ZUKOR, President, Paramount Famous Lasky Corporation of N.Y.

Famous Players Canadian Corporation 1927 board of directors.

its British and Canadian content. The majority of members of its board of directors were, after all, Canadian-born, or British-born in the case of financier Sir William Wiseman. The vast majority of the company's employees were also Canadian, and Famous Players presented several British and/or Canadian "road shows" that appealed to Canadians, including Canada's famous First World War concert party, the Dumbells.[74] The Dumbells returned to Canada after the war, became the first Canadian hit on Broadway, and toured the country a dozen times in the 1920s, including several stops at Famous Players theatres throughout Canada.[75] This support of Canadiana gave Famous Players an edge over the competition, including Allen Theatres Limited, which was struggling to survive.

As *The Film Daily* reported:

> J.P. Bickell and N.L. Nathanson, vice-president and managing director of Famous Players Canadian Corp., controlling Regal Films, Ltd., the big chain of Capitol Theatres across Canada and other enterprises, have not been idle. Announcement was made that the F.P. interests had made an offer of two-fifths of par value for the stock in Allen Theatres Ltd., and it was understood that this offer would be placed before the creditors at Toronto on 25 May. Famous Players made an offer of purchase last fall and negotiations were carried on for a considerable time.[76]

Though Famous Players was finding success, the relationship between Nathanson and Bickell would one day fall on hard times. Their relationship was one of the few that ended on bad terms for Bickell, who sold his interest in the company in 1929 after a bitter feud.[77] Nathanson was then fired by Adolph Zukor who had gained controlling interest in Canadian Famous Players.

Nathanson aside, J.P. generally enjoyed long years of good fellowship with the majority of his friends, many of whom were among the country's most important movers and shakers. One other very close friend of J.P.'s was R.S. "Sam" McLaughlin, a trusted companion as they sat on the boards of various companies and made several investments together. These include McIntyre Porcupine Mine, International Nickel Company of Canada (INCO), and Griffith Island in Owen Sound.

The Toronto Mining Exchange had an odious reputation, but the mining men were the high-living, hard-drinking diamonds in the rough Sam liked to chum with. So although J.P. was a generation younger, he and Sam became fast friends. The two went on a monthly junket to New York City, which would include a night on the town and a visit to their friend Billy Durant's favourite spot, the Cotton Club in Harlem.[78] Durant was the founder of General Motors.

These friends, all with wildly different personalities, skill sets, and spheres of influence, would help shape how Bickell would spend the second half of his life.

By 1920, however, the millionaire was still only thirty-six. That year he moved his mother Annie and his thirty-three-year-old

R.S. "Sam" McLaughlin, president of General Motors Canada, Bickell's friend and director of McIntyre Porcupine Mines.

J.P. Bickell's 1930 Rollston Stutz, purchased after selling his interest in Famous Players in 1929.

Home of J.P. Bickell in the 1920s on 55 Glen Road, in the Rosedale area of Toronto.

sister into 75 Crescent Road in Toronto's posh Rosedale neighbourhood. Bickell moved into 55 Glen Road South, also in Rosedale. J.P. enjoyed a very close relationship with both his mother and sister, taking them on many trips to various far-off destinations. The family saved many pictures from these trips, including very many of his sister — aboard his yacht, in the back of one of his Rolls Royces, or showing off her opulent wardrobe. Her older brother's connections in the motion picture business may have been beneficial as well when it came time to attend the world premiere of *Gone with the Wind* in Atlanta at the Fox Theatre on December 15, 1939, with her husband Reverend J.B. Paulin.

It had been an impressive journey for the smiling lad from a manse in Molesworth, but there were many miles yet to travel and many mountains yet to summit.

Marjorie Bickell sitting on a Rolls Royce in front of Bickell's Mississauga estate.

Risk

High Stakes

Bickell's penchant for gambling was not unusual in the world of high finance, team sports, and mining — but the man certainly did have a flair for the spectacular when it came to laying it all on the line. Though perhaps overselling the legend ever so slightly, the *Globe and Mail* eulogized: "It is said of him that, as a young man in his twenties, he could lose $400,000 in an afternoon without turning a hair, and make $500,000 the next."[1] Adding to this mythology is one legendary tale that expresses Bickell's fondness for chance, even at a tender age. When in New York on a trip, the then twenty-one-year-old Bickell took part in a high-stakes craps game with the notorious gambler Arnold Rothstein. By evening's end, Bickell was up $25,000. The furious Rothstein complained bitterly that Bickell had quit early without giving the losers (namely Rothstein) a chance to win back their money. In a flabbergasting display of bravado, Bickell placed his winnings back on the table and challenged Rothstein: "I'll roll you double or nothing."[2] Rothstein agreed. Bickell went home with $50,000.

Bickell found dramatic acts of flamboyance irresistible. He rarely withdrew when spurred on by a challenger in any forum. Moreover, Bickell was willing to take his opponent much further than the latter had ever intended. Many pretenders would gulp when J.P. posed his seemingly flippant but always deadly serious dare: double or nothing.[3]

One card game at the King Edward Hotel in Toronto would cause Bickell grief for decades. John Scully sought to collect a debt from Bickell resulting from a high-stakes poker game at one of the King Eddy's infamous private card events in 1911. In these rooms thick billows of cigar smoke wafted over the crackling badinage of big-time operators, mining men, prospectors, and brokers as they wagered big money well into the night.

Scully was not a big-time operator. He was an invited guest who claimed that whenever he lost he had to pay up in cash, while the other big shots — who all held accounts at the various brokerage firms that were represented around the table — simply transferred their winnings and losses via a secret XYZ account. One night, however, Scully did win. And he won big: $1,800, an enormous sum in 1911. Apparently, those present assured Scully that he would receive his money out of the supposed secret XYZ pool the following day. Unfortunately for Scully, the money never came. He spent years trying to collect, but over the decades the gamblers at the table that night all passed away. All, that is, except Bickell. While Scully never claimed that Bickell personally owed him the money, he tried to lean on Bickell so he'd come clean about the infamous XYZ account. As far as Scully was concerned, it was a "debt of honour."[4]

For the better part of thirty-five years Scully hounded Bickell at the Bank of Commerce in Toronto. The hounding was so relentless that Bickell finally took Scully to court on nuisance charges. The *Globe and Mail* reported on the court proceedings in 1946:

"You admit the debt, if any, is long outlawed?" Crown
Prosecutor W.O. Gibson asked him. "Yes." Mr. Scully
did, but he didn't seem convinced that 35 years made
any difference — "tomorrow" must come eventually.[5]

Scully's badgering Bickell about the alleged debt failed to produce the desired result — only the result that the judge bound
Scully over to keep the peace on his own bond of $100. Yet Scully
managed one last roll of the dice. The following year he took his
appeal for the old poker debt to court, where a Toronto judge
threw out the last-ditch effort to force Bickell's hand.[6]

The thrill Bickell got from a good gamble was not limited
to card games. Bickell was a sporting man, comfortably fitting
the early-twentieth-century archetype of a man of leisure. Speed
boats and yachting were central to Bickell the young man. For
example, he held memberships in the Royal Canadian, Columbia
and Thousand Island Clubs.[7] In May 1911, Bickell bought the
Nulli Secundus, a motor boat officially listed with the Royal
Canadian Yacht Club.[8]

In the late 1910s Bickell, alongside the American James
Simpson, raced high-speed motor boats. The duo won several
trophies. One such event saw their boat *Peter Pan VII* win the
Royal Canadian Yacht Club's Gold Cup, on September 2, 1915.
Six days later *Peter Pan VII* took the Fenton Gold Challenge Cup
for power boats in Toronto. As *Sporting Life* reported:

> The victor averaged better than 52 miles for the
> course, which was more than four miles faster than
> her speed in winning the race on Thursday. *Baby
> Doris* was second, almost nine miles behind the *Peter
> Pan VII*.[9]

With this victory Simpson and Bickell got to hold on to the cup
for a year.

J.P. Bickell and F.G. Ericson at the Thousand Islands Yacht Club Regatta, held on the U.S. side of the St. Lawrence River on August 25 and 26, 1920.

Bickell was also associated with the Toronto Syndicate, a group that built and sponsored racing boats in both Canada and the United States, including the hydroplanes *Miss Toronto I* and *Miss Toronto II*.[10] Not surprisingly, the Syndicate included some heavy hitters in the financial world. They included J.P.'s friend Alfred Rogers, the coal and cement baron, in addition to F. Ericson, Thomas Rea, S.A. Sylvester, Fred Miller, Cecil Allison, W.B. Cleland, and others. The Syndicate made several entries into various high-profile races on both sides of the U.S.-Canada border.

Bickell was given the charge of driving *Miss Toronto I* and was also counted on to lead the second incarnation of the boat into battle. The *Toronto Daily Star* had high hopes for *Miss Toronto II*'s chances for the upcoming 1920 summer season:

> If *Miss Toronto* stands up she will have a big season, and if she shows the speed the syndicates confidentially expect of her, she will be one of the best advertisements that Toronto has had since the days of Ned Hanlan.[11]

Indeed, it was a big season. At the Thousand Island Gold Cup in Alexandria Bay, New York, *Miss Toronto II,* with Bickell and Ericson at the helm, represented the Toronto Motor Boat Club.[12] In a trial leading up to the main race, *Miss Toronto II* showed just how fast she could be. It was, as the *Toronto Daily Star* confirmed, almost too fast:

> *Miss Toronto* showed such a burst of speed that when the driver, J.P. Bickell, tried to take her around the buoy she leaped clear of the water and shot J.P. overboard, that is all except his feet. F.C. Ericson who was with him, seized Bickell and throttled down the boat, but before he got him back aboard

Bickell swallowed enough of the St. Lawrence to make a fish pond.[13]

The two-man team would, however, rebound nicely from their rather wet trial, and in the end *Miss Toronto II* cruised to a significant ten-mile victory. Lou E. Marsh, one of Canada's all-time greatest contributors to the sporting pages, described the race:

> Jack Bickell, who was driving *Miss Toronto*, let *Arab* away in front with an idea of finding out quickly just what they had to face. *Arab* roared down the course a ball of foam, but when the Ericson-Bickell combination opened up with everything *Miss Toronto* had they slammed by *Arab IV* like Man o' War romping by a selling plater.[14]

In five minutes *Miss Toronto II* logged the fastest five miles ever recorded in competition up until that point. Marsh dubbed her "the mile-a-minute boat" and paid a playful compliment to the boat's skip and first mate:

> The boys have talked a mile-a-minute and better for years, but this is the first time it was ever actually accomplished under race conditions, and to do it Bickell and Ericson had to drive her over 70 miles an hour on the straights, for the turns were short and dangerous, and the regatta fleet so thick and the captains so foolhardy that Bickell dare not round the ends faster than 20 miles an hour.

In doing a five-mile lap in five minutes flat, *Miss Toronto II* set a new North American record, beating the one held previously by *Detroit III*.

J.P. Bickell and F.G. Ericson establishing a new speed record in Miss Toronto II.

J.P. Bickell and F.G. Ericson in Miss Toronto II *racing Bickell's Avro 594 Avian III airplane.*

Bickell's love of the water, however, extended beyond motor boating. J.P. also owned a steam yacht he named *Vacuna*. It was, as the *Star Weekly* confirmed, a familiar sight on Georgian Bay.[15] Subsequent to the *Vacuna* was the 132-foot *Miramichi,* which carried a crew of thirty-two men. This was an impressive boat, worthy of a millionaire mining magnate. When the *Miramichi* charted a course for a destination, it was news, as this blurb from Florida's *Evening Independent* attested in 1927:

> Possibilities of a visit to St. Petersburg this season by J.P. Bickell, nationally known financier and member of the firm of Thompson & McKinnon, and a party of Canadian and American financiers is foreseen by William O. Kennedy, Florida representative of the firm. Mr. Bickell is well known throughout Canadian financial circles, with headquarters at Toronto. Should he visit this city he will arrive aboard his yacht, *Miramichi*, which carries a crew of 32 men. Mr. Kennedy is corresponding with Mr. Bickell at the present time.[16]

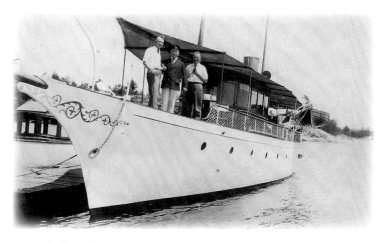

J.P. Bickell's yacht Vacuna *in Georgian Bay.*

Captain Bickell aboard his yacht Vacuna.

While it may not have been doing five-mile laps in hot pursuit of a challenger, the *Miramichi* was a calling card like no other, and its grandeur could, wherever it sailed, only announce the arrival of Canada's Sultan of Land *and* Sea.

High Times

Soon, Bickell would add Sultan of Sky to his calling card. To be sure, Bickell's sense of adventure suffused every aspect of the man's life. Nowhere perhaps was this more evident than in his love of flying. In the age of Charles Lindbergh and Amelia Earhart, flight was still the preserve of the elite of the elite; international flight was that much more so. But flying was well within J.P.'s reach, and given his love of the spectacular it was a natural fit.

In 1937, on the spur of the moment, Bickell flew to Shanghai from the United States. He did so mostly on a dare from his friend Ben Smith.[17] In an article on Smith, Forrest Davis of the *Saturday Evening Post* retold the supposed chain of events that led to the impromptu flight to China. It started while the two men were visiting San Francisco:

> Neither man had the haziest idea of going to China until, strictly as a gag, Ben pointed to the card, saying: "I dare you to fly to Shanghai tomorrow."
>
> "Let's see if they have space," Bickell replied.
>
> The ribber was ribbed. Ben's crest fell. He didn't want to go to China. Bickell is a Canadian; his passport was in Toronto; Ben's was at his estate at Bedford Village, Westchester County, New York. Bickell's private plane carried his passport to Chicago, where it caught the air mail. Over the telephone, Smith arranged with the State Department for a duplicate to be filled out in San Francisco.[18]

The trip was on. But it was hardly smooth sailing: Japan was already at war with China, a key episode in the prelude to the Second World War. By the time Bickell and Smith arrived in Shanghai, all planes had been grounded. No one was flying anywhere and the two men were stranded. So to get out, Bickell and Smith crossed Siberia to Moscow by rail, as the *Globe and Mail* attested: "They arrived in Shanghai just in time for the start of Japanese bombing. They got out to Dairen and started a long trek home, first across Asia on the Trans-Siberian Railway."[19]

As told by Jim Smith, Ben's son, "It was on this railway trip that the men were each assigned one towel for the week. Well, during the trip, every time Jack got up to do something, my Dad would use his towel to shine his shoes, and this got Jack very upset. They managed to laugh about this for years to come, and it was funny to hear them tell the story." Even in the most dire of situations the two men could share a good laugh.

The spur-of-the-moment flight garnered world press. It was a particularly fetching story because the hotel Bickell and Smith were staying at in Shanghai was destroyed by Japanese aerial bombing only two hours after the pair of adventurers checked out.[20] The trip added to an international-man-of-mystery persona that Bickell wore like a comfortable sweater.

Despite, or perhaps because of, its dangers, flying fully captured Bickell's imagination — and, as it happened, his money too. In 1938 Bickell sold his yacht and bought an amphibious airplane. It was an eight-passenger Grumman Goose G-21, constructed by McKinnon with the call letters CF-BKE. Almost immediately after purchasing it, Bickell flew to the Arctic.[21] While he did have a pilot's licence, Bickell seldom flew solo and relied on various expert pilots to take him where he wanted to go.[22]

China was far more than the thrill Bickell had hoped for. It had nearly cost him his life. Yet his luck held; he had already

J.P. Bickell boarding his private plane for one of his many adventures. Bickell stood by the motto "All work and no play makes Jack a dull boy," and had the proverb tiled above the mantelpiece at his Port Credit estate.

survived a string of near misses. In 1933, for instance, J.P. had to be rescued from a hunting camp near Parry Sound that had been frozen in. Then in May 1937, not long before the Shanghai incident, he was booked to fly to Germany on the doomed zeppelin *Hindenburg* — only five days after the day it burned to the ground. "They were actually on their way to Lakehurst, New Jersey, from Manhattan when the incoming *Hindenburg* burst into flames," as told by Jim Smith, Ben's son. There was an infamous cross-country trip in July 1938 with Ontario Premier Mitchell Hepburn, where Bickell and company were wrongfully presumed missing. In September of that same year, poor weather trapped Smith and Bickell's ship in a cove in Hudson Bay in northern Quebec while the men were on a polar bear expedition. And while serving with Lord Beaverbrook in the Second World War, Bickell and Beaverbrook were spared a watery death in the Atlantic Ocean when a last-minute crew switch altered the pair's flight plans.[23]

Bickell was undeterred. He would often fly on a whim, even to the more exotic and remote regions of the world. In August 1938, for instance, Bickell, alongside Ben Smith and pilot Jim McDonald, flew his enormous eight-passenger Grumman to Seal River in the Belcher Islands in Hudson Bay.[24]

Bickell's trademark generosity was always apparent. J.P. habitually parked one of his planes just outside the Air Canada gate and instructed Bruce Gibson who, in 1938, was a young pilot of only twenty-one, that "anybody who wishes to go up in the plane can go."[25] And Gibson dutifully flew several people, many of whom would otherwise never have had a chance to see the ground from cloud level. Perhaps even more generous were Bickell's actions at the outbreak of the Second World War. Bickell quickly donated his Grumman G21 to the RCAF, which took it on strength with the military serial 924 RCAF.[26] Bickell did have some issues with the initial terms. It was no secret that he was not a fan of the federal government of the day. As former

J.P. Bickell's Grumman G-21A amphibian, considered at the time to be the wealthy man's aircraft. The pilot, James Towne, is on the aircraft, while J.P. Bickell and Sydney Logan wait to board.

J.P. Bickell (second from right) joins Amelia Earhart Putnam on Eastern Airlines' Florida Flyer as guests of Eddie Rickenbacker to attend the Indianapolis 500 motor races, May 30, 1935. Additional guests were Ontario Premier Mitch Hepburn (sixth from left) and "Sell 'Em Ben" Smith (fifth from right).

auditor general and *Ottawa Journal* reporter Watson Sellar confirmed, Bickell was "not enthusing over the Cabinet in office."[27] Bickell's asking price had been a bit steep for those at National Defence, so he was finally persuaded by Henry Borden to donate the plane to avoid public criticism. J.P. was fine with the donation but wanted a promise that if and when he purchased a replacement, the plane could enter Canada free of duty and sales tax. That was the sticking point.

Regardless, Bickell's sense of duty to the nation prevailed and his commitment to the war effort on both sides of the Atlantic was unassailable. J.P. soon donated his other plane, a Grumman Goose G-21A, which became RCAF 941 on November 1, 1940. This plane would later become part of the Alaska Coastal Airlines fleet after the war.[28]

While the headaches and harrowing experiences associated with these still early days of flight might have turned off most people from future risk-taking, Bickell's sense of adventure seems only to have been electrified. "Smiling Jack" chose to fly regularly up until his death. In 1950, just one year before his death, Bickell and Smith flew from the south of France to Germany, where Smith had business to attend to, and then home via Tokyo, Alaska, and Edmonton. When the pair arrived in Toronto, they headed immediately to New York, where Bickell, as director, needed to attend a meeting for the International Nickel Company.[29] Such was the often unforgiving schedule that Bickell maintained. He wouldn't have wanted it any other way.

A Sporting Man

J.P. Bickell harboured a deep affection for the sporting life. For one thing, he was an avid golfer with a decent handicap who spent many cruel Canadian winters golfing in the sunny south. He also held a membership at the Mississaugua Golf and Country

Club in Port Credit. He loved the club so much that he even lent it fifty thousand dollars during the Depression just to keep it solvent.[30] The loan was set at 5 percent for ten years on the condition that the club balanced its budget every year.[31] The club's health and financial solvency was more than just a mere business arrangement for Bickell — it was a matter that struck close to home, literally: J.P.'s mansion actually flanked the Mississauga Golf and Country Club. Bickell wanted his home course and next door neighbour to succeed.

It is clear that J.P. never shrank from a challenge in his business affairs. The same might be said of his time on the golf course. On one occasion he was goaded by a party of wealthy American men with whom he was playing a round at the club. The stakes had been set at five dollars a hole. Throughout the day, the Americans kept up a line of trash talk about Canadians being "cheapskates."[32] By the time the group had made it to a particularly difficult hole, Bickell had had enough. He challenged his American friends to a *real* wager. Bickell proposed that the stakes for the hole should be five thousand dollars. The Americans could not possibly refuse after a long day of chirping, so they sheepishly agreed. "Smiling Jack" was soon five thousand dollars to the good.[33]

J.P. added yet another success on the links on the morning of August 15, 1925. It happened at his beloved course in Port Credit. No one had ever holed-out on the third at the Mississauga. That day Bickell was in a foursome with Hugh Johnston, T.W. Watson, and a gentleman named Mr. McClary. The third green, which sat considerably above tee-level, had a distance of 215 yards when Bickell aced it. Perhaps not surprisingly, J.P. chose to make a pretty big deal out of this special shot. And perhaps even less surprisingly, others would benefit from Bickell's stroke of good luck, as explained in the club's seventy-fifth anniversary book:

Club member J.P. Bickell, financier and philanthropist, made a hole-in-one on the third hole. To celebrate, he released eighteen coloured balloons from
the Club, offering $10 for the return of each balloon,
provided it was found outside a radius of two miles
of the Club. (He gave the finder of the balloon $4
and contributed the remaining $6 to the Star Santa
Claus Fund.) The fund received $108, indicating all
the balloons were retrieved. A hole-in-one party held
by Mr. Bickell at the Club raised a total of $179.30
for the fund.[34]

The *Toronto Daily Star* shared its pleasure of Bickell's generosity
with its readership:

> The poor children, as represented by the fund, are
> benefitting to the amount of $108. For this the
> thanks of The Star go out to Mr. Bickell and all those
> who assisted in the interesting celebration. There
> will be a great many little children made happy at

*Author Graham MacLachlan and Lea Hill, club member and archivist,
at Mississaugua Golf and Country Club, 2014.*

Christmas because the golfer succeeded in making
a "hole-in-one."[35]

J.P.'s love affair with the game endured, and in 1949, at age
sixty-four, Bickell won the "low net" in the Canadian Seniors
Association competition.[36]

Certainly, J.P.'s fondness for sport transcended the links.
Moneyed men of his vintage were often keen to support — and be
seen to support — amateur sports. This custom was a throwback
to old world sensibilities and a feudal spirit of amateurism: Lord
So-and-So would donate a trophy to serve as the prize in some
sort of competition in which the locals could square off against
one another. Whatever its origins, J.P.'s interest in the amateur
game was nevertheless sincere.

As in many urban centres across North America, boxing
thrived in Toronto after the turn of the century. Bickell showed
his support of the sweet science with a belt that he put forth for
Canada's featherweight champion in 1919. As the *Toronto Daily
Star* reported:

> J.P. Bickell, the well-known Toronto broker, racing
> hydroplane pilot and boxing fan, has offered a belt
> emblematic of the featherweight championship of
> Canada to the winner of an Eber-Atkins bout at 122
> pounds ringside.[37]

Whoever won the belt three times would, as outlined in J.P.'s
terms, become its final owner.

Hunting was also one of J.P.'s favourite pastimes with which
he liked to entertain his American friends, investors, and various dignitaries. In 1939 J.P. bought the twenty-six-hundred-acre
Griffith Island in Owen Sound, Ontario, as a retreat where
pheasants, deer, and Hereford cattle would be raised. He
formed Griffith Island Estates Inc., acting as the company's

president, and formed a syndicate with his friends Ben Smith, a New York stockbroker; Oshawa's R.S. "Sam" McLaughlin, of General Motors of Canada; Thomas Seagram, of Joseph E. Seagram and Sons Limited in Waterloo; Francis Farwell, president of Canada Coach Lines of Hamilton; J.L. Sullivan, a Texas oilman; and W. Anderson, a businessman from California.[38]

George Macauley, a reporter with the Owen Sound *Daily Sun-Times* who visited the island in 1945, estimated the pheasant population at twenty thousand: "The sky seemed to darken and a sound like thunder smote our ears as a flock of the birds rose from the ground directly in front of us," he wrote. "It would be impossible to be long on the island without seeing deer. The herd numbers in the neighbourhood of two hundred and it is not unusual to see forty to fifty of the graceful

Canadian Governor General Viscount Alexander of Tunis and J.P. Bickell wave as they leave the Big Bay dock for Griffith Island to hunt pheasants, Monday, October 30, 1950.

animals together at a time." Macauley described Griffith as "a hunter's paradise."[39]

This thrill of risk and love of sport informed Bickell's career trajectory and, more generally, governed the way the man approached life. Whether it was turning earth into gold or chasing down an opponent on the open waters, J.P. relished the idea of laying it all on the line. Yet despite his deep association with motor boat racing, golfing, and boxing, Bickell's name — at least when it came to sports — would become forever synonymous with the game played on ice.

Ice

Metal and Ice

Mining magnates and hockey men were, in many cases, one and the same during the early-twentieth-century mining boom in Canada. By now hockey had moved from the preserve of the upper-middle classes of the old century to the more win-driven attitudes that cut across class lines in the new century. Communities demanded victory from their squads. It therefore took someone with a strong will and and deep pockets to ice a winning team. High-stakes mining prospectors comfortably suited this role, and owning a hockey team was, for some, an important part of the mining magnate's portfolio. Toronto's Teddy Oke, for example, was a hockey player who made a mint in mining and later bought up several insolvent hockey clubs, including the Canadian Professional Hockey League's Kitchener Millionaires, and the junior squad, the Toronto Ravinas.[1] Bob Shillington, mining-man, druggist, politician, and top executive of the Ottawa Hockey Club, awarded his Stanley Cup–winning team of 1903 with silver nuggets, an act that gave birth to the team's legendary nickname: the Silver Seven.

Michael John O'Brien started as a railway builder but later went into mining and founded the town of Renfrew in the process. He established the O'Brien Silver Mine in Cobalt in 1903. While he was interested in hockey, donating the O'Brien Cup to the National Hockey Association (NHA), it was his son Ambrose who would thoroughly conjoin big-time mining with big-time hockey.[2] Ambrose founded not only the NHA, but also the Renfrew Creamery Kings (later the basis for the Toronto Blueshirts franchise), and, more famously, the Montreal Canadiens.

Before the NHA was established, the greatest hockey-playing mercenaries of the day were attracted to the lucrative, if unlikely, mining towns of northern Ontario. Founded in 1906, the Temiskaming Professional Hockey League (TPHL) boasted teams in mining hotspots such as Cobalt and Haileybury. The league, which lasted until 1911, was effectively a predecessor to the NHA, which itself later became the National Hockey League (NHL).

Remarkably, the TPHL was the first openly professional hockey league in Canada. (It was preceded by "Doc" Gibson's International Professional Hockey League of 1904–7 in Michigan.) The quality of the "hockeyists" that came to the north was thoroughly disproportionate to the modest size of the mining villages and towns in question. In 1910, for instance, Renfrew counted only three thousand odd souls, but its Creamery Kings hockey squad could boast superstars Newsy Lalonde, the Patrick brothers, Frank and Lester, and the peerless Fred "Cyclone" Taylor, who was paid an astonishing $5,250 for a twelve-game season (his salary surpassed that paid to Prime Minister Wilfrid Laurier).[3] Yet, despite O'Brien's best efforts and deep pockets, the Renfrew Creamery Kings, a.k.a. the Renfrew Millionaires, never won the Stanley Cup.

For many of the mining-magnates-*cum*-hockey-club-owners, the game was often a matter of one-upmanship: each trying to outdo one another by icing a better, trophy-winning side. And predictably, gambling dominated the culture of pre-war hockey. Stakes were high, gaming was rife, and spirits flowed freely.[4] Ultimately, the game was a reflection of those who invested in it. It is little wonder, then, that Bickell would soon throw his hat in along with the risk-taking dreamers.

Civic Pride

At first Bickell played only a peripheral role in professional hockey. Senior amateur hockey had not yet been eclipsed by the pro game. Industrial hockey, for instance, was popular in Canada's urban centres after the turn of the twentieth century. In Toronto, teams such as the K. & S. Tire Company competed for the Daily Star Trophy in the Toronto Industrial Association senior league. As one of the directors of the tire company, Bickell was involved in divvying out honours to the company team, which took the city championship in 1924.[5]

In a joint venture that same year, J.P. began to take baby steps toward the professional game. The forty-year-old Bickell, alongside N.L. Nathanson, led the partnership that bought the Toronto St. Patricks from Paul Ciceri, Charles L. Querrie, and the Hambly brothers, Fred and Percy. Querrie had been a popular lacrosse player who later transformed into a hockeyist. Before focusing on the popular newspaper column he later wrote, he also served as manager of hockey operations at the Arena Gardens, and he stayed on as managing director of the St. Patricks when Bickell arrived on the scene.[6]

When Bickell made his appearance in early December 1924,[7] he invested $25,000 into the St. Pats and mostly served as a silent partner.[8] Hockey Hall of Fame Honoured Member Frank J. Selke characterized Bickell's investment with the St. Patricks in the following words:

[Bickell] merely supported St Pats as a matter of civic pride and because of his friendship for Charles Querrie. Hockey was a small sideline with J.P. Bickell; while Querrie, who was astute enough to cope with any situation, did not have the funds with which to buck the well-heeled gentlemen from Montreal and the United States who were franchise-holders.[9]

It was this sense of civic pride and duty — not to mention a chance to compete with "well-heeled gentlemen from Montreal and the United States" — that kept Bickell interested in this "small sideline." While Bickell's sense of civic pride and deep pockets had assisted his friend Querrie, it also caught the attention of a fiery hockey man whose imprint on the game was paramount.

In 1926, Conn Smythe had just finished assembling a New York Rangers team that would become a perennial Stanley Cup contender, with assets that included the Cook brothers, Ching Johnson, and the supremely talented Frank Boucher. Inexplicably, the Rangers unceremoniously fired Smythe before his new acquisitions had played a single game. Smythe did not sit out of the game for very long, however. Immediately following his dismissal, Smythe targeted Bickell and approached him about getting in with his Toronto St. Patricks.[10]

When Smythe met with Bickell, he did not disguise his contempt for how the St. Patricks team was being handled. Neither did Smythe play coy when discussing who he felt should get the chance to right Bickell's sinking ship of a hockey squad; he wanted the job. Initially, Bickell was unmoved and instead chose sportswriter and hockey referee Mike Rodden to take over what today might be termed as the team's hockey operations.

It was a poor choice. Upon hearing of it, Smythe warned J.P. that Rodden would prove to be an unqualified failure. He was right. Only a few weeks later, Bickell, as sheepishly as his robust personality could manage, contacted Smythe to see if he was still up for the St. Pats job.[11] Smythe was. He also recognized an opportunity and decided to add nuance to his initial terms: now he wanted a share of the club. This gumption impressed Bickell, who perhaps saw a little of himself in the wiry and fiery veteran of the First World War. Smythe got his way.

While the mythology surrounding the Toronto Maple Leafs undersells Bickell's role and perhaps oversells Smythe's, the relationship between the two men remained generally amicable and had a profound influence on the course of the city's grand narrative. Events unfolded quickly. When a group from Philadelphia was willing to pay Bickell and company $200,000 to secure the rights to the club and its players and move the team to the City of Brotherly Love, Smythe, as the story goes, implored Bickell to refuse. Just as Querrie had before him, the fearless Smythe played the civic card on Bickell.

Certainly, in the years leading up to the Depression, Toronto was a city on the rise. The city had begun to flourish after the war. Toronto had become both central bank to Ontario's industries and and storefront for these industries, including the all-important mining sector, which was so close to Bickell's heart. Importantly, old Hogtown had surpassed Montreal as the nation's most important business hub. It was Bickell's duty, according to Smythe, to keep the team in Toronto. Regardless of who convinced whom and how, Bickell decided that the team should and would remain in Toronto.

There still remained the matter of fulfilling the necessary terms. For his part, Bickell agreed to hold on to his existing $40,000 stake in the club if Smythe could somehow pay off the remaining $160,000 for the other investors. On February 11, 1927, the *Toronto Daily Star* (though making no mention of Smythe), reported:

> The new owners of the local professional hockey club will take over the St. Patrick's [*sic*] franchise on

Monday. Mr. J.P. Bickell will be the president of the new company with a strong board of directors. The public will be invited to take stock in the new company, but most of it has been taken up privately.[12]

By St. Valentine's Day 1927, Smythe had sourced some financial backing with help from, among others, the stockbroker Ed Bickle and Peter Campbell.[13] Smythe and company were able to put down — with Bickell's crucial assistance — the first $75,000. Yet even though the team was staying put, changes were on the way.[14]

Badge of Honour

The St. Patricks nickname had been an unabashed attempt to charm Toronto's significant Irish population into the St. Pats' home at the Arena Gardens, often referred to as the Mutual Street Arena. The ploy enjoyed only mixed results. Many Irish-Torontonians were not moved and remained loyal to the city's more traditional Irish squad, the St. Michael's junior hockey team.[15] In truth, the St. Patricks brand of Irish green and vague Catholicity had been misdirected. Toronto was still very much an outpost of Protestant Britain, and this brand of Britishness thrived in a city where over 80 percent of the population was of British ancestry. Two-thirds of non-native Torontonians had been born in the United Kingdom, and 75 percent of the population claimed to be Protestant.[16] Anglo-Protestant tenets of propriety, thrift, and self-restraint were touted throughout "Toronto the Good." An enduring love affair with an English King and British iconography likewise persisted. It was an iconography that was pleasing to Bickell, who — given his own Scottish-English heritage — greatly revered the British and Canadian colonial traditions.

Further, the First World War had recently claimed thirteen thousand of Toronto's sons. The sacrifice remained very much in the consciousness of the "Queen City," where two-thirds of Toronto's eligible men (the highest rate in Canada) had volunteered to fight for King and country.[17] It was clear, at least from a business perspective, that any public charming should have been aimed at the staggering majority and not the fringe Irish population. It was also common knowledge that even the men who previously ran the St. Patricks had considered these facts and were respectfully considering changing the name to the Maple Leafs. But it took the tenacious Smythe, with the help of his benefactor Bickell, to make the move.[18]

The team's new owners promptly set about building a brand. They wanted to accessorize their new team with an iconography that was more in harmony with the sentiment that prevailed across the city. The majority, though they might not have known it yet, were ready to support a brand that was truly representative of their own sense of self: Union Flags, "God Save the King," royal portraits, odes to the Canadian effort in the First World War. It was this brand that opened up the hearts of the local population, and it was this brand to which the son of Reverend David Bickell gave his unreserved blessings.

Long before the nation's red and white flag was officially inaugurated in 1965, the maple tree and its leaves were already ubiquitous in Canada. French Canadians had adopted the maple leaf as a symbol in New France at the turn of the eighteenth century. The maple was, as Jacques Viger, Montreal's first mayor and president of the Saint-Jean-Baptiste Society attested in 1834, "the king of our forest … the symbol of the Canadian people."[19] By the late 1840s Toronto's pre-Confederation literati could boast a journal entitled *The Maple Leaf Annual*. It hardly surprises, then, that that journal referred to the maple leaf as the chosen "emblem of Canada" in 1848.[20] Five years on, in 1853, musician James Paton Clarke wrote his "Lays of the Maple Leaf" as part of a published work of poetry and music.[21] Clarke's ode bears testament to the fact that many among Canada's cultural elite were aiming to embed the maple leaf as a primordial element in the national folklore.

This same process was occurring within military circles in Canada. By 1860, for instance, the 100th Regiment incorporated the maple leaf into its regimental badge. That summer, the maple leaf was being used in decorations around the Dominion in anticipation of the arrival of the Prince of Wales (later King Edward VII), who landed in Newfoundland on July 24 to begin his North American tour.[22] Soon afterward the maple leaf became a symbol of Confederation; soldiers of the 100th Regiment paraded down the streets of Ottawa on July 1, 1867, with maple leaves fastened to their headgear.[23] Some forty years later the helmets of Canada's soldiers during the Boer War were likewise distinguished by a maple leaf.[24] This association between the maple leaf and the Canadian soldier was further strengthened during the First World War, a fact that had profound influence on for Bickell and Smythe's future team.

Perhaps more famously, Alexander Muir penned "The Maple Leaf Forever" to celebrate the new country in October 1867. According to Muir, he was inspired by a large maple tree that stood at Memory Lane and Laing Street in Toronto, where the composer lived.

> In days of yore, from Britain's shore,
> Wolfe, the dauntless hero, came
> And planted firm Britannia's flag
> On Canada's fair domain.
> Here may it wave, our boast our pride
> And, joined in love together,
> The thistle, shamrock, rose entwine
> The Maple Leaf forever![25]

The song served as Canada's unofficial national anthem between Confederation and the Second World War. The maple icon was hardly the preserve of Muir's Laing Street; it sprouted up everywhere. Ontario and Quebec, for example, both incorporated the maple leaf into their coats of arms in 1868; by 1876 the maple leaf also began appearing on Canadian coins.[26]

Predictably, the maple leaf found solid representation within sporting spheres. The Guelph Maple Leafs baseball team had been operating since 1861. They held on to the name until 1953. Hamilton too had its Maple Leafs Base Ball Club, which also commenced play in the 1860s. From the middle of the nineteenth century onward the nickname began appearing in sporting contexts throughout Toronto, including the Maple Leaf Cricket Club; the Yorkville Maple Leaf lacrosse club (which had been competing as early as the 1870s); the Maple Leaf Club of Parkdale; the Maple Leaf Curling Club in Scarborough (which was in operation by the late nineteenth century); and the Maple Leaf Stakes, which was a feature of the thoroughbred horse racing calendar from its inauguration in 1892.[27] Crucial to this narrative, however, was the Toronto Maple Leafs baseball team, which had been a successful franchise since 1896. Maple trees and leaves were entrenched elements of Canadiana and the nation's sporting teams many years before the hockey Leafs took to the ice.

The baseball Leafs were of particular import to the hockey incarnation. Indeed, the two teams were indirectly linked. By the time Smythe hooked up with Bickell to take over the St. Pats in 1927, the baseball Leafs were enjoying success in the International League (though perhaps not as much as in the 1950s when Jack Kent Cooke, yet another Bickell associate, took over the club). The baseball Leafs — who were adorned in the now-familiar blue and white — had long been filling their parks. These included Sunlight Park (Queen Street East and Broadview Avenue); Hanlan's Point Stadium (on the Toronto Islands); Diamond Park (in present-day Liberty Village); and, by 1926, Maple Leaf

Stadium (Bathurst Street and Lakeshore Boulevard). It was at Maple Leaf Stadium that the team won the Junior World Series in its first year at the new park.

Timing suggests that the hockey Leafs may have been inspired by the already successful baseball Leafs. The Leafs won their Junior World Series, after all, only one year prior to the St. Pats' take-over. Moreover, the baseball Leafs were owned by Lawrence "Lol" Solman, a prominent Jewish businessman in Toronto. Solman was also the managing director of the Arena Gardens, where the hockey Leafs played their first-ever home game. Crucially, Bickell had a minor interest in the Toronto Maple Leafs baseball team. These links undoubtedly helped to direct Bickell, Smythe, and company in their move to rename the St. Patricks.

While the Maple Leafs name was definitely associated with sporting success in the city, it was an emblem that shared even greater currency among Torontonians. As we have seen, the maple leaf was a cultural touchstone for a city that had, not a decade earlier, been so earnestly committed to winning the First World War. The maple leaf appeared often in regimental nick-names and on the troops' badges.[28] More concretely, the maple leaf represented military success for the nation, and in particular, victory at Vimy Ridge. In terms of reverence for and sentimental attachment to that "war to end all wars," Toronto was unlike any other city in Canada. Bickell and the Maple Leafs brass knew this. The group saw an opportunity in the maple leaf symbol. As Smythe explained:

> The Maple Leaf, to us, was the badge of courage, the badge that meant home. It was the badge that reminded us of all our exploits and the different dif-ficulties we got into, and the different accomplish-ments that we made. It was a badge that meant more to us than any other badge that we could think of, so we chose it, hoping that the possession of this badge

would mean something to the team that wore it, and when they skated out on the ice with this badge on their chest, they would wear it with honour and pride and courage, the way it have been worn by the soldiers of the first Great War in the Canadian Army.[29]

It is not known how much influence the success of the baseball Leafs had on the name change for the city's hockey team. What is verifiable, however, is that under Smythe and Bickell's stewardship, the royal-blue-and-white-clad hockey Maple Leafs became a team with a recognizable symbol of community pride that articulated the deep sense of self that was surging through the veins of Toronto's people.

Smythe chose his wartime crony, the legendary Victoria Cross recipient Lt.-Col. William "Billy" Barker, to serve as the Maple Leafs' first president.[30] Yet it was Bickell who really assembled the stunning off-ice management team. Their names read like a who's who of the Canadian business world; their inclusion ensured that the Maple Leafs would be a sound and well-oiled business machine. The board of directors of 1927 included:

- H.R. Aird, of Aird, Macleod & Company, Bond Dealers
- Col. Wm. Barker, V.C., D.S.O., M.C., President Lynedock Tobacco Co. Ltd.
- J.S. Beatty, Barrister
- J.P. Bickell, President McIntyre Porcupine Mines Ltd.
- E.W. Bickle, of E.W. Bickle & Co., Bond Dealers
- E.H. Blake, Barrister
- Peter G. Campbell, of Campbell, Stratton & Co., Members of Toronto Stock Exchange
- Allan Case, President Pease Foundry Company
- F.J. Crawford, of F.J. Crawford & Co., President Standard Mining Exchange
- Cecil Cowan, Vice-President Ontario Malleable Iron Co.

- M.S. Hass, Secretary and Director Geo. H. Hees, Son & Co.
- Blake Jackson, Jackson, Lewis Construction Co.
- W.A.H. MacBrien, Director Port Hope Sanitary Co.
- T.A. McAuley, President Arnold Brothers

By the time the Toronto Maple Leaf Hockey Club Limited went public, it had issued twenty-one thousand of its authorized thirty-five thousand shares. Though he wasn't listed on the official board, Smythe would soon become the public face of an impressive Maple Leafs management team, one that was built outward by its central architect, J.P. Bickell.

In the enduring narrative of the Leafs, Smythe's role has been exaggerated at the expense of Bickell's: the contribution Bickell made in assembling the pieces for Toronto's all-time most beloved franchise has simply been soft-pedalled. Yet Smythe had great respect for Bickell. The two shared many similarities. Smythe must have recognized the tenacity of a man who had succeeded in opening a brokerage firm at twenty-three and then left it to dive head-first into the unforgiving mining game. And J.P. too truly respected Smythe. Bickell was no doubt impressed by the man's ferocity and determination, and as a result he invested in Smythe, heavily and often. Without Bickell's backing, Smythe's Maple Leafs might have fizzled out in Philadelphia, a city that was perhaps not quite ready for top-flight hockey.[31] Under the Bickell-Smythe union, in its first year the new team generated $83,000 in revenue. In 1930 the Leafs brought in $123,000.

Despite these successes, the franchise was limited by its outmoded facility, the Arena Gardens. It was a matter on which Smythe again had to convince Bickell to take that great leap of faith. Back in 1927, Smythe helped persuade Bickell to keep the hockey team in Toronto as a matter of civic pride. Three years on, Smythe once again drew out the civic pride card. This time he had to convince Bickell and then a group of investors that a new arena was absolutely necessary for the future growth of the franchise. With the country and the world still reeling from the stock market crash of a few months earlier, many thought Smythe was dreaming. He was. It just so happened that his friend J.P. was a dream-maker.

Cornerstone

In the 1920s, hockey culture, at least at the professional level, began to put on a "high hat."[32] NHL teams had outgrown the old barns they were housed in, and owners wanted to attract a greater cross-section of people by jettisoning the more undesirable elements associated with hockey-watching, such as rowdy behaviour, drunkenness, and gambling. With the Montreal Forum being built in 1924, followed by New York's Madison Square Garden the next year, Smythe and his board of directors, with Bickell at the helm, knew well that the Maple Leafs had to leave Mutual Street.

Opened in 1912, the Arena Gardens was already lacking in several ways. While it was only the third rink in the country to have artificial ice, the official listed capacity was only 7,150, much lower than the newer NHL rinks that started to appear in the 1920s. Moreover, the rink was sadly lacking in comfort. With no heating in the building, and only basic wooden benches serving as the best seats in the house, the Arena Gardens was never going to provide the dream venue that Smythe, Bickell, and company had envisioned.[33]

Maple Leaf Gardens was designed to take the hockey experience to a new level for spectators, and also to attract a more genteel clientele. The kinds of fans the partners wanted in their rink were put off by the rough and tumble, gambling-heavy, alcohol-bathed environment that defined the game at the time.[34] Brawls in the stands were nearly as commonplace as on the ice, and sometimes

the two were not mutually exclusive. So deficient were the barriers
between spectator and player that fans could reach over and grab
a sweater or throw insults, programs, and just about anything
they could lay their hands on at the players. "Arena patrons," as
Frank Selke confessed, "accepted accommodation in those days
that would have utterly appalled a theatre crowd."[35] Yet it was
precisely that crowd whom Smythe and Bickell wanted to attract.

Alcohol, not surprisingly, played a huge role in setting the edgy
atmosphere at Mutual Street, and many fans were well lubricated
long before the opening face-off. This habit was not limited to
the fans. When he was running the St. Patricks, Charlie Querrie
had the unenviable task of retrieving many of his players from the
local bootleggers before a game.[36] Many players drank not only
on game day, but actually during the game.[37]

Bickell and Smythe wanted to get away from the "bear pit"
cliché associated with the old arena and the game in general.
For his part, Conn Smythe envisioned Maple Leaf Gardens as a
place with "class":

> a place to go all dressed up … we don't compete with
> the comfort of theatres and other places where people
> can spend their money. We need a place where peo-
> ple can go in evening clothes, if they want to come
> there from a party or dinner,… a place that people
> can be proud to take their wives or girlfriends to.[38]

Along these same lines and speaking to the hopes for elevating the hockey-watching experience, Bickell later wrote the fans
a letter entitled "President's Address to Sports Followers of the
Queen City." In it, he observed:

> The enthusiastic support of our patrons during the
> past few years encouraged and warranted us in provid-
> ing enlarged, better-planned and more comfortable

quarters. The citizens of Toronto and the country surrounding have always given generous support to clean, well-organized athletic activities, and we are confident in the hope that our management will continue to merit a patronage commensurate with our expanded effort.[39]

Actually getting the comfortable quarters built, however, took a bit of doing.

To start the buzz, Smythe had Foster Hewitt plug the idea of a new arena during his broadcasts from Mutual Street's Arena Gardens. It planted a seed in the minds of hockey fans that something big was coming to the city. Sports columnist Ted Reeve, writing under the pseudonym Nutsy Fagan, offered what he felt was the driving force behind the new arena and why it was so necessary:

> Civic pride demands it.… Have we not in this grand and glorious hamlet the Canadian National Exhibition, the tallest skyscrapers in the British Empire [the Royal York was the tallest building in the Empire at this time], the most beautiful race track in North America (Woodbine not Dufferin), government control, the University of Toronto, and the Balmy Beach Canoe Club? The answer is, 'Yes, we have the Canadian National Exhibition, the tallest skyscrapers in the British Empire, etc.' We have all these and many more remarkable and prepossessing public institutions, and why, then should we be curtailed to a theatre of thump that will only hold eight thousand people with one foot in the aisle?[40]

Thanks in large part to Bickell, hockey fans in Toronto would not have to wait long.

The building of Maple Leaf Gardens in less than six months in the heart of the Great Depression was an incredible achievement and required a Herculean effort from many committed individuals. Its very existence is now solidly and rightfully part of Toronto's grand historical narrative. There were, of course, some rough patches along the way. While Bickell believed that he had proven his civic duty, and had given the Maple Leafs and the proposed new arena enough of his dollars, he was railroaded into coughing up even more than he was prepared to. Larkin Maloney, general manager of Canada Building Materials, helped Smythe to sell the idea of the Gardens to his former boss, Bickell's friend Alfred Rogers. Bickell had invested in Alfred Rogers's St. Mary's Cement Company. Then as now, the Rogers family was one of Canada's most influential and wealthy families.

Maloney encouraged Rogers to buy a significant block of stock in the Maple Leaf Gardens venture. After doing his bit, Rogers called Bickell and told him that he'd just unilaterally invested another ten thousand dollars of J.P.'s money in the Gardens. Bickell was fit to be tied. He remonstrated with Rogers and told him that he had already invested twenty-five thousand, which was quite sufficient. Rogers apologized but politely told "Smiling Jack" that it was too late and that he simply couldn't back down now.[41] Soon afterward Smythe visited Bickell. The latter had, by this point, reconciled himself to the idea of going another ten large in on the project. In the end, J.P. told Smythe that while he thought the money would be lost for good, he and Rogers believed in him and, at the very least, they were doing their civic duty.[42]

However, not everyone was on board the Smythe train from the outset. Eaton's College Street department store, for instance, wielded a significant influence over the building of the Gardens. Eaton's wanted the block around its store to remain within the existing aesthetic of a retail district. In fact, the owners of Eaton's were not sure whether or not they wanted a hockey arena so close to their store. They had to be convinced several times that the Gardens would add value and not detract from the street, and would attract the right quality of consumer. Eaton's itself was trying to attract "civilized" bourgeois customers, the very same patrons that Smythe, Bickell, and the Leafs wanted to bring through their turnstiles.[43]

Eaton's nevertheless continued to interfere in the Gardens' planning. It wanted the Leafs to take an inside lot on either Wood Street or Alexander Street. But the Leafs, with Bickell in the vanguard and with the support of the Montreal-based architectural firm Ross and Macdonald, knew well the importance of securing the Church and Carlton lot, with a strong presence in the existing retail district.[44] Still, Eaton's fought the Leafs all along the way, and its owners ended up having a disproportionate say in a new hockey rink that wasn't theirs. The Gardens' lead architect shared the arena's drawings and specifications in order that "the T. Eaton Company should have the privilege of reviewing the plans and specifications so that we might endeavour to make any modifications that they might suggest."[45] This caveat went some way in mollifying the department store's executives.

Yet, Eaton's was not the Leafs' only headache. There was also a Mr. Charles G. Carmichael, who owned the lot at 60 Wood Street. It was the only lot on the property that Eaton's did not own. While the lot was worth approximately ten thousand dollars, Carmichael was holding out for the astronomical price of seventy-five thousand dollars.

The business team that Bickell helped Smythe assemble, however, was too powerful to stop. There were simply too many big fish involved for Eaton's — or anyone else — to refuse to play hockey. As mentioned earlier, the coal and cement baron Alfred Rogers had joined Smythe and Bickell, as had Rogers's colleague Larkin Maloney. The team had likewise secured the Sun Life Insurance Company and an elite architecture firm in

Ross and Macdonald. That particular firm had been responsible for Ottawa's Chateau Laurier, the Royal York Hotel, and the grand Union Station in Toronto, and, perhaps most importantly, Eaton's store on College Street.[46] Beyond logistics help from Sun Life and Ross and Macdonald, the Leafs had the services of stockbroker Ed Bickle, as well as Bickell's friends and representatives from the Bank of Commerce, the William Wrigley Company, the British-American Oil Company, the Bank of Nova Scotia, Algoma Steel, the CNR, Canada Life, Simpson's, and of course the powerful, if unenthusiastic T. Eaton Company.[47] Bickell helped Smythe access all of these solid connections, including sourcing the much-needed steel to build Maple Leaf Gardens at a time when it was in short supply. The dream-maker had delivered.

At precisely 2:30 p.m. on September 21, 1931, a document was buried underneath the cornerstone of the brand-new arena. It was, after a fashion, a time capsule that explained the specific events and details related to the construction of the spectacular arena:

> The foundations of the structure throughout are carried to hard clay, in some instances, through twenty-six feet of water bearing sand. The main structure is of reinforced concrete design from the footing up to the top of the seating.... The design of the roof is quite unique. It consists of two trussed arches spanning 308 feet diagonally from corner to corner and meeting in the centre of a four way pin or intersecting spheres.... The structural design is also made by the Engineering Department of Ross & Macdonald, under the efficient direction of Mr. G. Townsend, in co-operation with the Engineering staff of the Dominion Bridge company on the steelwork, and the Engineering Department of the

Truscon Steel Company of Canada on the Concrete Structure. The General contract for the construction of the building was let to Thomson Bros., Limited, on May 29th, 1931, and the first game is to be played in the building, November 12th, 1931.[48]

The whole process was made possible in part by the teams that worked twenty-four hours a day, as the document explained:

> It is worthy of note as a demonstration of the confidence of the public at large in the Directors of The Maple Leaf Gardens Limited, and the popularity of the Maple Leaf Hockey Team under the management of Mr. Conn Smythe, that every workman engaged on the structure subscribed to stock in the venture. Never in the history of organized labour in Canada had the Unions as a union agreed, on behalf of their men, to accept a portion of their wages in stock of the venture on which they are working.[49]

In the end, 1,200 labourers laid 750,000 bricks and emptied 77,500 bags of concrete, and got the job done on time.[50]

Conn Smythe was grateful for Bickell's help in the process. Many years later, shortly after Bickell died, Smythe shared his feelings with popular *Toronto Daily Star* sportswriter Milt Dunnell: "You could say, without exaggerating, that Bickell was the cornerstone of the whole project."[51] Part of the reason J.P. was the cornerstone of the project was his ability to shake down the necessary cash to cover unexpected costs. Bickell called in many favours to help facilitate this grand dream.

Maple Leaf Gardens cost approximately $900,000, fully $150,000 over the projection — a figure that was going to jeopardize the much-needed mortgage. Milt Dunnell recalled:

It was Bickell, according to Smythe, who replenished the pile of blue chips for the hard-pressed Garden dreamers. He had the right connections among the people with folding money, and he went to work on them. He would call up some person he knew, and he'd tell this person what we were doing. Then he'd say that we needed $175,000 in a hurry, and he'd tell the party at the other end of the line how much he expected from him. That's how we got the money we had to have when we were threatened with failure.[52]

In short, Bickell's campaigning saved the new dream ice palace, and J.P. was named the first president of Maple Leaf Gardens.

When the cornerstone was laid, a group of dignitaries, including Bickell, William MacBrien, Ed Bickle, Ontario's Lieutenant-Governor W.D. Ross, Reverend Dr. John Inkster, and Victor Ross, were among those present. Bickell addressed the crowd that had gathered:

This building, with which I trust your name will be long associated, perhaps might be regarded as a civic institution, rather than a commercial venture, because its object is to foster and promote the healthy recreation of the people of this British and sport-loving city. It represents the combined efforts of all sections of the community. Capital for its creation has come very largely from those who are actuated by a spirit of civic patriotism, rather than a desire to reap financial benefit. No less a high ideal has inspired those who labour in creating it, for I am glad to tell your Honour that the members of the various trades employed are becoming part-owners of the enterprise by accepting a

J.P. Bickell (right) laying the cornerstone of Maple Leaf Gardens with Lieutenant-Governor W.D. Ross (left), September 22, 1931.

substantial portion of the remuneration in stock. There is I believe no precedent in any similar project for this happy situation.[53]

Without Bickell's stamp of approval, not to mention his gold mine holdings in Schumacher and elsewhere, Smythe might never have realized his dream of building hockey's "Mecca." And how like Mecca would the Gardens seem to hockey fans everywhere!

November 12, 1931

Public *spaces*, including sports spaces, have often articulated power relations that exist between class, gender, and sometimes race. They are viewed by some as a sort of disciplinary tool where the working and lower classes could, by attending, acquire more civilized habits by imitating their "betters."[54] Maple Leaf Gardens was no different. Smythe and Bickell had been clear: they hoped that it would make hockey-watching more appealing to women and to a more desirable clientele than that what was found at the Arena Gardens on Mutual Street.

Certainly, the Gardens distinguished class by virtue of selling tickets in sections that possessed varying degrees of comfort. The most expensive box seats, for instance, were opera-styled armed seats, padded with red leather. The next section offered wooden seats with wooden backs and arms. The top sections provided only long wooden benches. Adding to the distinction between sections (and classes) were the men's washrooms, which were porcelain lavatories on the main floor, compared to the infamous stainless steel troughs of the cheaper sections. And by virtue of the boxes and rail seats of the lower levels, it was difficult to move between sections.[55]

Likewise, even though ladies were welcomed, especially to offset the previous uncouth norms found in hockey culture, less than 13 percent of the Gardens' washrooms were allocated for women's stalls.[56] Hockey arenas were still, it seemed, a predominantly masculine space.

The Gardens was also very much a British space. Given Bickell's fondness for the British and the fact that Canada was still, at least in many ways, a satellite of Great Britain, this was no accident. Old Orange Ontario was alive and well in the arena. A portrait of the King, musical odes courtesy of the 48th Highlanders, not to mention the Leafs' royal blue and white colours all connected the team to the Anglo-Protestant sensibilities of the city. Toronto was, after all, still very much attached to all things British.[57] At the same time, the Leafs' lineup boasted a fair share of hometown boys. In these ways, Toronto saw its own reflection in the Gardens' ice.

The Gardens was officially opened on November 12, 1931, in a sold-out game between the Toronto Maple Leafs and the Chicago Black Hawks. Before the puck dropped on that momentous evening, Bickell was among the speechmakers who expressed his vision for the building, a vision that saw hockey as only one of the rink's uses. It was a rough go for J.P. The impatient crowd interrupted Bickell's speech with booing and rafter-calls to get the game under way. Frank Selke recalled the incident in his autobiography, *Behind the Cheering*:

> J.P. Bickell, the President, justifiably proud in having helped Smythe and his associates put over the new deal in tough times, decided to make a speech. Knowing that sports crowds hate long talks, J.P. first fortified himself with a few extra belts of Scotch to counteract the heckling. He had prepared a rather lengthy address and he was determined to finish it, despite the catcalls and admonitions to "Play hockey!" which came from every corner of the building.[58]

In hindsight, the Leafs could have reconsidered the number of speeches that preceded the game. Apart from Bickell's, these included efforts from Ontario Premier George S. Henry, Toronto Mayor William Stewart, directors Ed Bickle and George R. Cottrelle, NHL President Frank Calder, and radio celebrity Foster Hewitt.[59] Toronto's print press did not miss the opportunity to draw attention to the crowd's chatter and irritation at the speeches of these notables. Edwin Allan, sports columnist for the *Mail and Empire*, for example, believed that the incident was caused by "younger elements" in attendance, and Bickell and the others were "entitled to a better reception."[60] Similarly, the *Toronto Telegram*'s J.P. Fitzgerald opined that "it is certainly deplorable that prominent men like the Premier and the mayor should be subjected to the howls of the impatient rabble."[61] The *Evening Telegram*'s Ted Reeve added a little levity to the incident when he referred to the awkward speeches on opening night as "two minutes' silence in respect of the shareholders."[62] Some forty years later, in the 1970s, Foster Hewitt himself enjoyed a poke at Bickell's address when he was involved in an audio recreation of the Leafs' opening game on an LP produced by *Hockey Night in Canada* and the Longines Symphonette Society. Hewitt made a sportscast-style comment on Bickell's "long speech that has had the crowd on edge."[63]

Despite the reception, Bickell was not put off trying to articulate his and Smythe's vision for respectable behaviour at the Gardens. In a 1934 program Bickell advised:

> To the patrons may I suggest that they match the players' skill and energy with their cheers, so that when the game starts, dull care departs, and entertainment such as no other game provides, will be our lot.[64]

Bickell continued to promote "respectable" public behaviour so that watching a game at Maple Leaf Gardens was far removed

28

President's Address to Sports Followers of the Queen City

J. P. BICKELL, ESQ., President Maple Leaf Gardens

THIS season the Maple Leaf Hockey Club is really "At Home" to its friends and supporters for the first time in a new Arena, embracing in its construction all modern improvements and facilities, and generally recognized as the finest of its kind in the world.

The enthusiastic support of our patrons during the past few years encouraged and warranted us in providing enlarged, better-planned and more comfortable quarters. The citizens of Toronto and the country surrounding have always given generous support to clean, well-organized athletic activities, and we are confident in the hope that our management will continue to merit a patronage commensurate with our expanded effort.

We confess a certain measure of pride in presenting this year's team, knowing that win or lose they will continue to give their supporters their best efforts. With no inclination to underestimate the strength of opposing teams, we believe the Maple Leafs will finish at or near the top. Indeed, in this splendid Arena, inspired by the generous cheering of their many supporters, we expect that they will rise to the occasion and bring back to this City the Stanley Cup, emblematic of the World's Championship. In short, we hope that when the season ends we may bracket the team with the Gardens and describe them both as "The Best in the World".

"President's Address to Sports Followers of the Queen City" — J.P. Bickell addresses Maple Leafs fans on the Gardens' opening night.

6

The "Gardens" Executive

Harry M°Gee G.R. Cottrelle J.P. Bickell E.W. Bickle Conn Smythe

Directors of Maple Leaf Gardens, Limited

SIR JOHN AIRD
MR. J. P. BICKELL
MR. E. W. BICKLE
MR. J. E. BIRKS
MR. G. R. COTTRELLE
MR. A. L. ELLSWORTH
MR. GEO. H. GOODERHAM

MR. R. A. LAIDLAW
MR. W. A. H. MacBRIEN
MR. LEIGHTON McCARTHY
MR. HARRY McGEE
MR. F. K. MORROW
MR. J. Y. MURDOCH
MR. FRANK P. O'CONNOR

MR. ALFRED ROGERS
MR. FRANK A. ROLPH
MR. VICTOR ROSS
HON. W. D. ROSS
MR. R. HOME SMITH
MR. CONN SMYTHE
MR. JOHN A. TORY

The page from the Maple Leaf Gardens Opening Night Program highlighting the Gardens' board of directors.

from taking in a Toronto hockey match in the drunken gambling barns of previous times.

It was not always "respectable," however. In 1937, for instance, the *Toronto Telegram* spoke to the "boys in the wagering ring — on the east side behind the blue section."[65] This was the infamous bullring that lasted until just after the Second World War. How far the Gardens had evolved from the arena on Mutual Street was, perhaps, a matter of how close you sat to the bullring.

Taken on balance, though, Maple Leaf Gardens was an enormous success. The arena that Bickell helped make a reality was home to many championship teams: eleven Stanley Cup championships for the Leafs, including one during their very first season in the new building.

The Gardens also provided Toronto with an A-list venue for international musical icons such as Elvis Presley, the Beatles,

The Toronto Maple Leafs versus the Boston Bruins, November 9, 1933. Lining up with the players are Lieutenant-Governor Herbert A. Bruce, J.P. Bickell, and NHL President Frank Calder.

Frank Sinatra, Bob Marley, and Bob Dylan. Political rallies, religious events, sports of all sorts, and a variety of shows and cultural entertainments were all staged at the Grand Old Dame on Carlton Street. These uses, not to mention the iconic position that Maple Leaf Gardens still holds on the nation's cultural landscape some fifteen plus years after its main tenant played its final game there, would have no doubt put a smile on the face of "Smiling Jack."

After the Second World War, Conn Smythe was in a position to truly take over Maple Leaf Gardens. Since he had climbed on board with the St. Patricks, Smythe, who was a director, had become the public face of the franchise. The truth, however, was that with such a powerful board of directors, Smythe's powers were marginal. But by 1947 Smythe had finally become the powerful force behind the Leafs that he had always wanted to be.

The process was sped on by the sheer success of the Leafs and, more specifically, by Bickell's influence. Bickell's friend George McCullagh was also one of Smythe's allies. He and Bickell were part of the pack that ran with Ontario Premier Mitchell Hepburn. Smythe's ascension was partially facilitated when McCullagh was installed as vice-president. There was also the matter of securing enough shares in Maple Leaf Gardens. Stockbroker Percy Gardiner was a particularly important part of the transition for Smythe when he sold Conn thirty thousand shares in Maple Leaf Gardens at ten dollars each. This was quite generous on Gardiner's part, as the Gardens' shares were worth far more than this. With the newly acquired shares Smythe could now exercise the control over Maple Leaf Gardens that he had long dreamed of. Yet, it was Bickell, a 20 percent owner of the club, who was central to the entire process and who wielded his significant influence on behalf of his pal Smythe.

J.P. Bickell, Globe and Mail *publisher George McCullagh, future prime minister Lester Pearson, Ontario Premier George Drew, and a friend at the Maple Leaf Gardens office before a game.*

While Bickell may officially have been only a director, his position in the business of the nation meant he cut a wide swath. With Bickell championing him, Smythe won his long sought-after majority control of Maple Leaf Gardens. Conn Smythe was eternally grateful for Bickell's help, and more than once referred to him as one of the best friends he ever had.[66]

November 19, 1947

In J.P. Bickell fashion, it was not clear whether Bickell sold or gave his shares to Conn Smythe. Either way it was his significant ownership share, power, and influence that put Conn in the position he sought.

At a board of directors meeting held on November 19, 1947, to acknowledge Bickell's long-standing contribution and to signify the transfer of power, the board presented Bickell with an inscribed sterling silver cigar box. Just below the engraved Toronto Maple Leafs logo it bore the following inscription:

Presented to
J.P. Bickell ESQ
by
***The Directors of the Maple Leaf Gardens
as a token of appreciation of his long
and valuable services as Chairman,
President and Director.
Toronto, November 19, 1947***

In another demonstration of their heartfelt appreciation and in addition to the inscription, the personal signatures of all twenty board members were inscribed in their own handwriting:

E.W. Bickle	James Murdoch
G.R. Cottrelle	W.A.H. MacBrien
F.J. Crawford	C.G. McCullagh
A.L. Ellsworth	W.F. Prendergast
P.R. Gardiner	Alfred Rogers
Ian Johnson	Sigmund Samuel
R.A. Laidlaw	Conn Smythe
S.H. Logan	John Tory
R.C. Mathers	N.C. Urquhart
F.K. Morrow	J.J. Vaughan

J.P. Bickell stayed on the board as a director until his death in 1951.

The J.P. Bickell Memorial Award

With J.P.'s untimely death and to perpetuate his friend's memory (and perhaps also to reward Maple Leafs players who were perennially and suspiciously passed over by the NHL during awards season), Smythe established the J.P. Bickell Memorial Award (a.k.a.the J.P. Bickell Memorial Cup) in 1953. It was given to those within the Maple Leafs organization who demonstrated a high standard of excellence, though it wasn't awarded every year.[67] The *Globe and Mail* proclaimed the award's arrival:

> One of the world's finest and most unique sports awards in its design, the gold masterpiece will perpetuate the memory of the late J.P. Bickell termed by President Conn Smythe as "the cornerstone of the whole project" in building of Maple Leaf Gardens. First recipient will be named next month at a board of directors' meeting.[68]

Team captain Ted Kennedy became the first recipient of the award. Bickell's sister Marjorie presented the ten-thousand-dollar trophy to Kennedy prior to the Leafs' season opener. The fourteen-karat gold cup was mounted on a silver base and was specially made by the Jensen firm in Copenhagen.[69] Kennedy was allowed to keep a miniature of the trophy, which was also made of fourteen-karat gold.[70]

The following is taken from the October 11, 1952, Toronto Maple Leaf program (the Leafs versus the Boston Bruins), which highlights the announcement of the cup to the Leaf faithful.

The late J.P. Bickell, described by Conn Smythe as "the corner-stone of the whole project," in the erection of Maple Leaf Gardens, was a man of enormous wealth and paradoxical simplicity.

He began life humbly, became one of the world's greatest financiers in dazzling, almost overnight rapidity, had the world in his hands, so to speak, yet never once forgot his humble beginning. Rich but plain. A man of wealth, often called the richest man in Canada, who lived quietly, shunned the spotlight, masked great deeds under a preferred cloak of anonymity.

There never would have been a Maple Leaf Gardens had it not been for J.P. Bickell, and when he died Aug, 22, 1951 an integral part of the Gardens seemed to have been taken away.

* * *

That's why plans were made for something unique to commemorate a man who was to phrase it simply, unique. Gardens' directors decided on a trophy.

They wanted a trophy that would embody the richness of Bickell's Canadian background and the simplicity of the man and to make it an award that would constitute one of the greatest moments in the life of the individual selected as its winner.

It would be a Maple Leaf trophy, to be awarded to a Leaf player for performing with such a high standard of excellence that he would be truly a great member of the team, just as Mr. Bickell was. The awarding of the trophy would be left to the discretion of the directors. It could be won for tremendous feats over a season or over a period of years.

In short, a player winning the J.P. Bickell Memorial Cup would have to be one who had in him the characteristics of the man who the trophy honours.

***

The T. Eaton Co. was commissioned to handle the creation of the J.P. Bickell Memorial Cup. Mr. G.M. Gray was given the assignment of getting a design that would stress the rich Canadian background of Mr. Bickell and still portray the simplicity of his life.

[In] the design world today, apparently, one firm in particular, is ranked as par excellence. That is Jensen (pronounced Yensen) of Copenhagen. That is where Mr. Gray went, coupling a business trip for his firm with a visit to Jensen. As a result of that mission, Harald Nielsen, chief of Jensen's design board, personally undertook the task.

The accompanying photograph of an artist's conception of the finished product presents what could be termed one instance where a picture does not tell more than the proverbial thousand words. The J.P Bickell Memorial Trophy will have to be seen to be appreciated.

Valued at $10,000, which makes it one of the costliest of all sports trophies, the Bickell Memorial Cup consists entirely of 14-karat gold on a silver base. The replica, which will become the property of the player given the award, also will be of 14-karat gold, and is valued at $500.

***

If you study the picture of the trophy, this is what you will see:

A 14-karat gold cup, with gold maple leaves at each side and a gold maple leaf superimposed on gold hockey sticks on the facing; a neck with an intricately created design, all in gold, which represents the true fruit of the Canadian hard maple tree; a gold ring bearing the inscription, and a base of pure quartz taken from the upper level of McIntyre Porcupine Gold Mines, the mining property which Mr. Bickell nursed through difficult days and made in to one of Canada's greatest. On the lip of the quartz base are 20 gold maple leaves, on which will be inscribed the names of the cup-winning individuals. The cup will be set on a base made from maple.

Over a year of planning has gone into the designing of the J.P. Bickell Memorial Trophy and it will be several months before Jensen will complete its fabrication. It will be one of the most beautiful and most

Members of the Toronto Maple Leafs board of directors look on at the newly created J.P. Bickell Memorial Award: (from left) F.J. Crawford, Conn Smythe, W.A.H. MacBrien, Ed Bickle, and George McCullagh.

First presentation of the J.P. Bickell Memorial Award, October 1953. Marjorie Bickell Paulin, J.P. Bickell's sister, congratulates Ted Kennedy as W.A.H. MacBrien and Balmer Neilly, president of the McIntyre Porcupine Mine, look on.

Johnny Bower being presented with the J.P. Bickell Memorial Award by Ontario Lieutenant-Governor Earl Rowe, 1960.

expensive sports trophies in the world and it will be the only one of its kind. Assurance has been given that the design, which has been copyrighted, will not be used for any other purpose. [71]

Harold Ballard made one interesting point of note about the cup in a 1977 interview. "It never was meant to be given out annually," Ballard pointed out. "There were three earlier years when nobody got it. Yes, you can say the standards have been raised. I'd say the directors are looking for something along the lines of a Stanley Cup." [72] With that, after being the foundation of an organization that won seven Stanley Cup championships between 1924 and 1951, the cherished cup commemorating a man who meant so much to so many, and became the cornerstone of the entire project, slowly faded into obscurity.

March 4, 1999

The closing of Maple Leaf Gardens came with an outpouring of emotion from everyone who had grown up in its presence. It was also fondly remembered by the Honourable Senator Frank Mahovlich as he stood up in the Senate Chamber to read an address parts of which are paraphrased as follows:

> Honorable Senators, today I should like to speak on the closing of an institution.... In the process of raising the money needed to buy Maple Leaf Gardens, Conn Smythe knocked on the door of J.P. Bickell, who had also built the McIntyre Arena in Schumacher, where he was the CEO of the McIntyre gold mine. I mention the McIntyre Arena, honourable senators, because that is where

The J.P. Bickell Memorial Award.

The J.P. Bickell Memorial Award at centre ice, Air Canada Centre, 2015.

I was born as a hockey player. It was there in Schumacher that Bickell built the community centre for the use of all miners, to entertain and be entertained, so that morale would be high in that northern community.

To honour J.P. Bickell, the board voted in favour of having a "most valuable" trophy, which is, to this day, one of the most prestigious that a Maple Leaf player can win. Conn Smythe is honoured by way of a trophy for the most valuable player in the Stanley Cup playoffs. That trophy is a copy of the Maple Leaf Gardens.

The last game at the Gardens was played on February 13 with 104 former players present, of which I was one. It was ironic that the Chicago Blackhawks were present at the end, because they were at the beginning and won both times. [73]

4

Extravagance

Bickell the Banker

There was, of course, a fair amount happening outside of Bickell's hockey life. Indeed, J.P. was in the swim of many divergent socio-economic and cultural currents. The year 1928 was a particularly busy year for Bickell, who was named a director of the Canadian Bank of Commerce.[1] Bickell had gotten out of the brokerage game to concentrate on McIntyre Porcupine but was now keen to get back in. This was fairly easily done. Bickell's significant American business ties readily led him into a position in the Thomson and McKinnon stock brokerage camp, members of the New York Stock Exchange.[2] Outside of their New York office, this high-end brokerage firm also had offices in Jacksonville, Miami, and Chicago.[3] A.W. Thomson passed away and R.W. McKinnon retired in 1929, allowing Bickell to become a senior partner.[4] In this new position Bickell would routinely make, and sometimes lose, as much $500,000 in a single day. There were more gains than losses, even during the Depression, and these allowed Bickell to open another Thomson and McKinnon office in Sarasota in December 1937.[5]

The Thomson McKinnon Building, Miami Beach, 1930 — J.P. Bickell's Florida office.

Also in 1928, the forty-four-year-old Bickell became an elected director of the International Nickel Company of Canada. J.P. truly put this company on the map. McIntyre Porcupine was, after all, one of the largest investors in International Nickel, and most of this investment had come before Sudbury's Frood Mine had proven its weight in nickel.[6] It was a shrewd move for Bickell. International Nickel stock increased fully ten times in value.[7]

On the eve of the desperate Depression, Bickell was sitting pretty: a multi-millionaire mining magnate and now bank director who was truly entrenched in the elite level of high finance. As the *Northern Miner* opined, Bickell was able to amass one of the larger Canadian fortunes through

> shrewd, longsighted investment, pursued with an almost stubborn perseverance and dependence upon his own personal judgement. "J.P." always got all the information possible about any proposition, and had an uncanny faculty for stripping things to their essentials. His approach to a speculative venture was

The International Nickel Company Organization (INCO) board of directors, September 28, 1948.

purely speculative. In his approach to an investment he demanded it should be everything an investment should be, and more. The fact that his company's investments changed little throughout the years indicated his ability to choose wisely.[8]

It seemed that Bickell's Midas touch for choosing wisely was infallible, as his wealth continued to accrue.

In 1931 Bickell and Chicago speculator Thomas M. Howell were able to win big on corn. In July the United States Department of Agriculture forecast a bumper corn crop. This declaration meant that there would soon be a drop in the price, so sellers obviously sought to move their corn before it lost its value. By extension, there were "bears" who speculated that they would be able to buy back the corn they had sold in August for a bargain price. Bickell and Howell didn't see it that way. The duo remained unconvinced by the Department of Agriculture's forecast and so bought all of the corn that was on offer. On paper, the pair owned over eight million bushels of corn, a number that exceeded that year's entire delivery demand for the United States.

The duo was right on the mark. There was an absolute crop failure. Those same "bears" had to come to Bickell in August to buy back the corn they had sold, now priced at fourteen cents more per bushel. As the *Sandusky Register* somewhat blithely reported:

> Up-to-date rivals of the Patriarch Joseph of ancient Egyptian renown brought to success today grain trade operations involving millions of bushels of corn. Thomas M. Howell of Chicago and James P. Brickell [*sic*] of Toronto, Canada were generally credited tonight with having emulated the achievement of Joseph of old in getting possession of the available corn supply needed in a crisis at a particular time and place.[9]

With this Chicago crisis, Bickell and Howell managed a profit of $1 million on the corn they had secured from short sellers.[10]

Bickell had an uncanny knack for choosing friends and associates who would invariably end up making a great deal of money together with him. One such friend was Sydney H. Logan, who was born in Debret, Nova Scotia. Formerly a hundred-dollar-a-year office boy in Halifax, Logan went on to become president and chairman of the board of the Canadian Bank of Commerce.[11] He was with the bank for several years and served as its senior agent in New York. In 1937 Logan was named president. Seven years later, in 1944, he was elected board chairman. As of 1938 Logan was also a director for Maple Leaf Gardens. Conn Smythe said of him, "I have found that in those days there were giants in the finance and business world, and assuredly he was one of them."[12] Just as assured was his good friend J.P. Bickell. Logan's daughter Anne attested to the closeness between Bickell and her father:

[Their friendship] became well known and led to various mutual directorships with one often suggesting the appointment of the other. You could not ask for two more divergent lifestyles, but possibly understanding of this, coupled with a mutual respect for ability led to the friendship. 'J.P.' had everything, but my father had a quiet place at Shanty Bay which he adored. It was here that Mr. Bickell came when in his last weeks he did not feel strong enough to pursue his normal hectic life.[13]

A cartoon of S.H. Logan "fishing from his bank" and Mr. J.P. Bickell "flying past".

J.P. Bickell and Sydney Logan cartoon.

Sydney Henry Logan, president of the Canadian Bank of Commerce and close personal friend of J.P. Bickell. The two men served on the board of directors for Maple Leaf Gardens Limited, Imperial Life Assurance, National Trust Company, Victory Aircraft, and the Canadian Bank of Commerce.

The two had met in the early days in the Cobalt silver strike, and their friendship was further galvanized when Logan was sent to Toronto. Though Anne's memories have been largely filtered through her mother Hilda (née White) Logan's recollections, Anne believed, just as Smythe and Smith did, that Logan considered J.P. Bickell to be his best friend.[14] Bickell and Logan were poised to become wildly wealthy in their respective pursuits. The story seemed to be repeating itself. Bickell's interests had strong roots, and the branches produced fruit without fail. By the 1930s there were very few people in North America whose net worth could match that of the reverend's son from Molesworth, Ontario.

Just Call Me "Mitch"

Bickell's inner sanctum comprised a very elite group indeed. While the list included the absolute *crème de la crème* of the North American business world, and celebrity sportsmen such as Conn Smythe, it was a colourful and slightly volatile politician who would be central to Bickell's interests during the Depression. Mitchell F. Hepburn, popularly known as "Mitch," was Ontario's Liberal premier from 1934 until 1943. An onion farmer, Hepburn had been a member of the United Farmers of Ontario before declaring for the Liberals. He was flamboyant, a convincing orator, and incredibly quick-witted. When forced to stand on a manure spreader to address a crowd at a country rally, Mitch quipped that it was the first time he had to give an address on a "Conservative platform."[15]

Hepburn's duality was, to many including Bickell, in equal measure remarkable and frustrating. He was at times a reformer, sympathetic to the farmers' and railway workers' causes, and at other times a reactionary, siding with the owners of Oshawa's General Motors during a labour strike in 1937. Hepburn is described by biographer John T. Saywell:

> Hot and impulsive, incapable of imposing restraint on his private life, and hyperbolic in speech and behaviour, he lived on the edge of his physical and emotional resources. Ontario has preferred leaders who had a firm grip on the tiller or, some would say, who used the brake more than the accelerator. Mitch Hepburn held the tiller of his public and private life with a light hand, and his foot sped from brake to acceleration with a seemingly carefree and sometimes dizzying abandon.[16]

Mitch often "sped from brake to acceleration" in the company of J.P. Bickell.

Hepburn had significant ties to various business sectors, leading many pundits during this volatile time to question the optics of some of his political decisions. Mitch was often scrutinized for the care and favour he gave to his "millionaire friends."[17] Many Depression-era Canadians began to question whether or not the main political parties and their leaders were simply doing the bidding of big business. Over time, many who had supported

Mitch wondered if he answered to his constituents or to friends such as Bickell. The Liberal Party had, nevertheless, been afforded the advantage of not being in office when the Depression hit. Despite his indiscretions, Mitch was able to attract a diversity of voters across the province, and especially in Toronto. These voters wanted a change from the status quo: Toronto had been a Tory stronghold for many years. Hepburn, as a "wet," was able to win the support of one significant part of the population, those invested in ending the age of temperance and once again allowing the sale of alcoholic beverages.[18] His platform also attracted Catholics (perhaps encouraged by his association with friend and Bickell associate Frank O'Connor), Italian immigrants, Toronto's small black community, Poles, and an assemblage of others who did not find the Conservative message to their taste.[19]

It was no secret that few men had better access to the premier than did Bickell. This brand of intimacy between Ontario premiers and mining moguls was certainly not new. Sir Oliver Mowat, Ontario's Liberal premier from 1872 until 1896, favoured heavy investment in the north. It paid huge dividends: the resulting return for the province was approximately seventeen million dollars. And so began a love affair with the mining industry that allowed the Ontario government to become debt-free in an unusually short period. Indeed, to be on the right side of the ledger at the turn of the century was no small feat when one considers that most other provincial governments in this new country were still burdened with large deficits.[20] This shared history between mining and ministering was not lost on either Hepburn or Bickell, and both men were hoping for the same happy results that Mowat's era had produced.

As Liberal premier in an age that would eventually introduce the economic philosophies of John Maynard Keynes and the so-called Keynesian Revolution, Mitchell Hepburn remained an economic conservative. This suited Bickell. Especially when one considers that as the Depression dragged on, the general consensus was pushing to move off the gold standard, a proposal that Bickell bitterly protested. To achieve his ends, Hepburn worked closely with seemingly odd partners, including Quebec's premier and head of the Union Nationale party, Maurice Duplessis. The Duplessis years were a period that many Quebeckers refer to as the Great Darkness. For a while, Mitch and Duplessis successfully resisted several federal initiatives that included railroading the introduction of various social programs. Importantly, at least as far as Bickell was concerned, the Hepburn-Duplessis tandem was able to delay the implementation of economic regulations such as Keynes's pre-scribed counter-cyclical proposal. This strategy called for the state to stabilize the economy during downturns by increasing expendi-tures, lowering taxes, and inflating the money supply. The strategy had been adopted by many governments around the world, but Hepburn was wary of policies that might redistribute wealth *away* from Ontario.[21] His friend J.P. agreed wholeheartedly.

The King Eddy

As the broker who had made his fortune with McIntyre Porcupine, Bickell topped the list of Hepburn's key associates, and Bickell's approval of Hepburn's policies was vital to the health of the province's Liberal Party. Still, Bickell wasn't the only one. Alfred Rogers was in the Hepburn sphere of influence, as were Percy Parker, an officer of both the Mining Corporation of Canada and Maple Leaf Gardens, and Frank O'Connor, owner of Laura Secord Confections Limited and a Maple Leaf Gardens board member. The business interests of these men, however, intersected with Bickell's at several junctures. It was a tight group of movers and shakers that was not so easily moved or shaken.

The group often frequented the Liberal Party bastion that was the King Edward Hotel in Toronto. The Ontario Liberal Association (OLA) held important meetings and conferences at the King Eddy. The hotel was, however, also home to the bacchanals and often not-so-discreet behaviour of its Liberal and vaguely libertine guests. The married Hepburn's unrepentant behaviour with regard to alcohol and women was infamous. Hepburn's exploits both amused the Conservative Party and armed it with a great deal of political ammunition.

The King Eddy is conveniently located on King Street between Victoria and Toronto Streets, a stone's throw from Yonge Street. Not much had changed at the hotel since Bickell attended those high-stakes poker games in the 1910s. Hepburn was particularly fond of the location given its propinquity to his closest wingmen: just around the corner was George McCullagh, the man who had arranged the merger that gave birth to the *Globe and Mail* in 1936 and was a strong ally of the Hepburn camp.[22] Close, too, was Liberal MP and barrister Arthur Slaght. And J.P. Bickell's downtown office was only a few blocks away. The hotel's centrality persuaded Mitch Hepburn to keep a hundred-dollar-a-month

J.P. Bickell with Ontario Premier Mitch Hepburn, George Cottrelle, and "Sell 'Em Ben" Smith.

suite there. Another friend, Frank O'Connor, followed suit and kept a room at the King Eddy. Together, this collective formed a sort-of Liberal Party rat-pack with Hepburn in the centre, flanked by his enigmatic millionaire friends.

Certainly, Hepburn's "rat-pack" was in many ways a group of masters that the premier would invariably have to serve or, at the very least, mollify. Fortunately for both men, Hepburn's and Bickell's viewpoints were usually complementary. Hepburn, for instance, battled on Bickell's behalf to lessen the federal tax levy on the gold mines in Ontario.[23] Yet although Hepburn had the support of Thomas Crerar, minister of mines, it proved difficult to implement tax concessions for depletion and exploration while Prime Minister Mackenzie King's reign was intact. (Incidentally, Crerar, like Bickell, was also born in Molesworth, Ontario; in 1920 he had been selected as leader of the then-influential Progressive Party.) The very public and sometimes ugly relationship between Hepburn and King did not serve the greater good, and the tension between Laurier House and the King Eddy was palpable.[24] As a result of federal policies toward the mining sector and the acrimonious relationship between the prime minister and Bickell's friend the premier, Bickell did not give King his unwavering support. This had consequences when war broke out.

Hepburn's close association with the likes of McCullagh, Smith, and Bickell gave life to a variety of rumours, half-truths, and the occasional pronouncement that was spot-on. While the King Eddy offered a strategic place from which to run the business of Ontario, it also offered a haven where Hepburn could, and often did, get up to no good. As Saywell confirmed:

> Mitch enjoyed the relaxed and carefree environment … with good drink. Harry Johnson feared that Mitch's indiscretions were politically dangerous and others, such as Paul Martin, found the excesses distasteful, but Mitch seemed unconcerned about the possibility of scandal.[25]

The British journalist Sir Anthony Jenkinson wrote about what he witnessed at the King Eddy during his time with Hepburn. After Mitch greeted Jenkinson at the door, he introduced the journalist to his friends:

> They were his doctor and a member of his government and two attractive girls who sprawled on a sofa and called the Prime Minister "Chief" and who generally lent an unparliamentary air to the place. A big broad-shouldered fellow with the supple movements of a trained athlete mixed drinks…. It was evident that he acted as a sort of bodyguard-*cum*-gentleman's servant to the Prime Minister. The latter called him "Eddie," but the girls called him "Bruiser."[26]

Hepburn drank to excess. An in-joke among journalists was that while whisky went to some men's heads, in the case of Mitch, it went to his penis.[27] So, while he may have loved his wife Eva, Mitch found a place in his heart for others. He took one mistress to Frank O'Connor's Scarborough farm, as well as to Bickell's Port Credit mansion where the couple was made welcome.[28] Considering his lot as a multi-millionaire bachelor with a penchant for fast cars, fast planes, and the fast life in general, it was unlikely that Hepburn's playtime offended J.P. in any real sense. It must be remembered that Bickell was, as Saywell diplomatically put it, "not known for turning down a drink."[29]

And then there were *the lassies O*. While J.P. never married, he certainly did not deny himself the company of women. There were several women in Bickell's life, some of whom even worked together, as Anne Logan explained:

> There were three women that he was particularly fond of. They were all nurses at the Wellesley Hospital, all at that time. And when mother [Hilda Logan] would

go with my father [Sydney Logan] to New York on business, which he did quite a bit, J.P. would ask her to buy silk stockings for the three lady nurses.[30]

Given Bickell's close relationship with her father Sydney, Anne came to know these three women:

I knew them all … and then after he died, mother was a very compassionate and sympathetic person and she would have them up at the [Logan] cottage every summer as long as they were alive and have them there together.[31]

In a strange way, Bickell's choice to remain a bachelor may have been in part due to the various sham relationships he witnessed among some of his dearest friends. As Anne Logan speculated:

He didn't have the time to settle down and give it a fair chance. He was too much of a roamer and a rover. He knew he wasn't marriage material. It may have been that [J.P.] had that amount of ethics that Mitch didn't have and some of the others didn't have, that he wasn't going to subject any woman to that lifestyle.[32]

Still, "Smiling Jack" was not prepared, as Anne Logan observed, "to deny himself the ladies."[33] While J.P. lived and died a bachelor, he was only very seldom without female companionship, right through until his declining days.[34]

Mississauga Mansion

Bickell revelled in his life in the fast lane. Anne Logan confirmed that J.P. "never gave anyone a bottle of champagne, he gave them a magnum of champagne."[35] The *Northern Miner* confirmed after Bickell's passing that J.P. was "bold and courageous in pleasure."[36] His twenty-room estate in Mississauga was a suitable playground for a millionaire mining magnate. The mansion was, according to the *Toronto Star*'s Stan Davies, "the scene of some of the wildest and most opulent parties outside of Hollywood."[37]

J.P. purchased the land that overlooked the Mississaugua Golf and Country Club from Alfred Morrow in 1921.[38] At that time the land likely included a cottage, but Bickell soon had the property radically altered. First, he commissioned John MacNee Jeffrey, a theatre architect, to alter the property by adding a major addition in 1922. The real changes came later with the famous Canadian architect Murray Brown, J.P.'s friend. As a journalist for the magazine *Construction* said of Brown in 1927:

> The writer of this article has no hesitation in saying that the progress of Murray Brown will be a deciding factor toward the development of the Canadian

J.P. Bickell's Port Credit residence, known as "Arcadia," featured in Construction Magazine, *May 1927.*

J.P. Bickell standing in front of the entrance to his residence in Port Credit.

Architecture of the future — toward that high goal of achievement to which his fellows have ever striven and will continue to strive until the record be completed.[39]

Brown, who also helped design theatres for Bickell and Nathanson's Famous Players, developed plans for Bickell's estate that included several expansions, among them a service building, an eight-car garage for J.P.'s cars, and quarters for the chauffeur.[40] Brown's work was completed in the Spanish Eclectic style, as described in a 2007 Corporate Report undertaken by the city of Mississauga:

> Both Classical and Prairie features are often incorporated into the Spanish Eclectic style. This mode, also known as the Spanish Colonial Revival, in its purer form, was popularized by San Diego's Panama-California Exposition. It was common in California but had Canadian examples in cities such as Vancouver, Ottawa and the Toronto area.[41]

Bickell's estate had a frontage of two hundred fifty feet and a depth of forty feet. His lavish villa also included a two-storey

The opulent swimming pool at J.P. Bickell's Port Credit residence.

dining room, a twenty-two-foot-high Great Room, a music room, a living room, a smaller dining room, several multi-purpose rooms, nine bedrooms, seven baths, a bowling alley, an indoor pool, an elevator that ran through the central tower and serviced three floors, and a personal movie theatre in which J.P. was often able to screen films before their public release.[42]

An award-winning fifteen-by-seventeen-foot library in the eastern pergola was completed in 1927. *Construction* lovingly described the library in detail in an article that was published the same year the room was completed:

> This room is entered through the music room and the panelled lobby by a very wide door, which door is leather covered; the material being sewn on and secured with special brass studs, the hinges being also of brass of strap type. This hardware, including the ring lock, have [*sic*] an antique finish and were imported from England. The room itself is approximately seventy feet long by sixteen feet wide, the far end being terminated by what is known as the Octagon, containing a large stone fireplace with overhanging breast supported on stone brackets. The ceiling of the Octagon is of ornamented plaster. Wrought iron grills on walls cover the radiator enclosures, and also provide ventilation for the theatre below. The main portion of the room has an open roof with structural beams supporting balusters, which in turn carry the apex of the roof. All bookcases and panelled recesses, also panelled wainscot and radiator enclosures, are of black walnut simply waxed and left to tone. The walls and ceiling of main room, also walls of Octagon are finished in antique thumbed plaster, painted and finished with an asphaltum glaze. The painted beams and inscriptions in the main room, also plaster ceiling of Octagon were

painted from designs prepared by Mr. A. Scott Carter. The floor is the original quarry tile of the pergola.[43]

Alexander Scott Carter was a famous heraldic artist. Hiring Carter and Brown — two men who were among the best in their fields — added another layer of prestige to the already impressive Bickell estate. A western service building was built in 1929, connected to the main house by an unusual underground tunnel.[44] This may have been part of the secret passageway that was known only to Bickell's nearest and dearest, and was certainly not mentioned in any of the official paperwork related to the mansion that Jack built. The passageway acted as a safeguard for Bickell; as Anne Logan observed, "if he was finding you a bit boring, he could just excuse himself and disappear into the next room."[45] The western half of Bickell's mansion was added in 1931. At a time when the average Canadian family's income was $4,000 a year, the mansion cost Bickell $250,000.[46]

J.P. Bickell's library, home office, and study, May 1927.

An English visitor at the Bickell estate recounted his experience there in an article in the *London Daily Express*:

> Mr. Bickell has just the house a bachelor should have. There is a long library with painted beams, and downstairs there are a swimming pool and bowling alley.… He has a Chinese cook called Joe, and a very good cook he is too. Not only does he prepare the food, but apparently he makes the beds, cleans the windows, and runs the house generally, and answers the phone with wisdom and discretion. The house is furnished with *objets d'art* and antiques acquired during years of search and contains a number of works of old and new painters for which Mr. Bickell, who is a director of the Grange, has been the successful bidder in many parts of the world. Two years ago he purchased after a stiff fight which ran the price into five figures, the world-famous Aubusson tapestries, since exhibited in Toronto galleries.[47]

Bickell's estate was bursting at the seams with priceless art, most of which found its way to the Art Gallery of Ontario upon Bickell's passing.

When Bickell died, Allen Rosen, a mining financier who made his fortune with United Asbestos, bought the property from the estate's executors in 1952 for approximately $150,000.[48] The Bickell mansion was later home to Stuart Bruce McLaughlin, who established Square One in Mississauga's city centre. McLaughlin bought the property in 1973. Before the building was successfully designated under the Ontario Heritage Act in 2007, the estate came up on the market in 2005 with a price tag of $4.9 million.[49]

Labour

Bickell and Hepburn's friendship transcended politics, and the premier regularly attended his friend's opulent Hollywood-esque parties in Mississauga. J.P. was heavily invested in the Liberal Party and had donated significant sums toward the party's election campaigns, but the fact is, he was genuinely fond of Mitch.[50] On more than one occasion the pair would take off in Bickell's plane to get away from it all. When the parliamentary session concluded in 1935, for example, Bickell's private plane carried Hepburn south to Miami where Eva Hepburn and the couple's children joined him for a month in the sun.[51] Bickell also flew Hepburn up to Timmins in May 1936 along with Donald McAskill (then president of International Nickel), and the men stayed with the ever-reliable mine manager R.J. Ennis.[52] Though Hepburn took some heat for flying about with his millionaire friend, theirs was a fellowship that endured.

Shared political perspectives fortified the fellowship between the two men. Communism enjoyed some support in Canada during the miserable heart of the Depression. Though declared illegal in 1931, this ideology captured the imagination of many workers and many of the unemployed.[53] Only 17.3 percent of workers in Canada's labour force in the 1930s belonged to a union.[54] The hard times saw an increase in the interest in trade unions, though, and an increase too in the militancy associated with the Canadian brand of organized labour.

The Workers Unity League (WUL), under the direction of the Communist Party of Canada, was one union that had made inroads with various trades, including miners. In accordance with the direction of the international organization for communist unions, the WUL gave way to the new American federation of industrial unions, the Congress of Industrial Organizations (CIO).[55] It was the CIO that would cause the biggest headache for Mitch Hepburn and, by extension, J.P. Bickell.

The CIO had been quite effective in Nova Scotia, pushing employers to engage in collective bargaining with certified unions. Yet, while Nova Scotia's premier Angus L. Macdonald opened a dialogue with the CIO, his Liberal counterpart in Ontario was not prepared to do the same. Biographer John T. Saywell was fairly charitable in explaining that Hepburn was no "enemy to organized labour." He was instead, according to Saywell, squarely against communist-tinged unions. The United Auto Workers (UAW), inspired by the "communist-tinged" CIO, called a strike that saw four thousand workers walk out of Oshawa's General Motors plant in 1937 on J.P.'s friend and fellow McIntyre Mine board member, R.S. "Sam" McLaughlin. In response, Mitch called on Ottawa to send in the RCMP, but Prime Minister King's government refused to intervene. This refusal prompted Mitch to send in his own "Hepburn's Hussars," or, as they were also known, "Sons of Mitches," to break up the strike. In the end, General Motors' Canadian managers engaged the UAW for negotiations.[56]

The CIO, led by John L. Lewis, had a clear goal to organize the unorganized. This meant establishing unions in the automobile, steel, rubber, and textile industries, as well as in the mining industry. This was obviously a matter close to Bickell's heart. Hepburn was resolutely against Lewis's union gaining the same strong foothold it had in Nova Scotia. In 1937 Hepburn warned that as long as he was Ontario's premier, Lewis "and his gang will never get their greedy paws on the mines of northern Ontario."[57]

Bickell and the other mine owners made it clear that they wanted the CIO to be stopped. Bickell promised Hepburn that if the CIO struck in the north he would shut down McIntyre Porcupine "until the men are ready to go back to work."[58] So tight-knit was the group of mining owners that other owners were expected to follow suit if Bickell had to follow through on his promise. Hepburn's uncompromising resolve to thwart the CIO was, it was thought by some, directly calibrated to the influence that his powerful, gold-mining, millionaire friends commanded in the political sphere.[59]

Regardless of prevailing optics, J.P. and Mitch's relationship continued to evolve. The two men flew in Bickell's private plane to take in the second Louis-Schmeling fight at Yankee Stadium on June 22, 1938. While the bout was a historic one with racial undertones and worth the trip (African-American boxer Joe Louis beat the white, German-born Max Schmeling), some Canadian pundits saw Hepburn's trip as the beginning of a calculated political adventure. Shortly after New York, the two men touched down to visit Duplessis before setting out for a cross-country trip. The *Toronto Star* echoed prevailing suspicions in Ottawa that the Bickell-Hepburn trip in reality signalled the creation of a new federal political party that was independent of King's Liberal Party.[60] Though he was perhaps not as convincing

J.P. Bickell and Premier Mitch Hepburn in front of Bickell's Grumman G-21A amphibian.

as he would have liked, Hepburn publicly denied throughout the trip that he had any intention of gauging the market for a new splinter party. Hepburn told reporters that while he was not a fan of Mackenzie King, he was a Liberal and had no intention of starting up a new political brand.[61]

While such suspicions might not have been altogether misplaced, there were other concerns that came up on the trip. Bickell's twin-engine Grumman amphibian departed Toronto for what was scheduled to be an eight-thousand-mile trip that included stops in western Canada and the Arctic Circle. Ben Smith joined Bickell, Hepburn, and their pilot for the trip. Bickell had brought Smith into Hepburn's circle. As "one of the shrewdest, coolest and most to be feared market operators," "Sell 'Em Ben" suited Mitch's gang. As Saywell attests, Smith "was as earthy in life as he was fearless on the street and was usually included in the northern hunting and fishing expeditions that looked like small encampments, with a dozen tents and nurses to attend the wounded."[62] These men left

Premier Mitch Hepburn (right) greeting "Sell 'Em Ben" Smith (left).

Toronto on July 17, 1938, and, with short stops in Sault Ste. Marie and Port Arthur (now part of Thunder Bay, Ontario), arrived in Winnipeg that same Sunday evening.

Upon arrival, Hepburn was once again forced to deny that his and Bickell's trip was in actuality a secretive political operation: "I don't want to be misinterpreted. I repeat that, in spite of what Toronto papers have stated, I am not on any political mission."[63] Still, in Regina, the men lunched with Saskatchewan's Liberal Premier William Patterson and the popular Liberal ex-premier James Gardiner. Such a meeting only added to the growing suspicions. J.P. had some familiarity with ex-premier Gardiner, as his first cousin William Paris (W.P.) MacLachlan had served as an MLA in James Gardiner's caucus. From Regina, Bickell's plane headed on to Edmonton, then north to Yellowknife, Port Radium, Fort Norman, Aklavik, and then south to Dawson City and on to Carcross. In Yellowknife, Bickell served in his role as a bank director for the Bank of Commerce's newest branch, an eight-by-ten-foot log cabin.

William Paris (W.P.) MacLachlan, first cousin to J.P. Bickell.

Staffing the counter, Bickell acted as teller, helping Hepburn and Smith open accounts at the branch.

At Carcross, a telegraph operator warned Bickell and company of poor weather. Initially ignoring this warning, the Bickell party set out for Juneau, Alaska, in what became a serious snowstorm. With a zero-zero ceiling, the plane was forced to turn back to Carcross. It was a frightful journey through a narrow gulch in the mountains, during which Mitch thought he heard the wing tips scrape the side of a mountain. The pilot was nevertheless able to bring the plane down safely.

The people awaiting the plane on the Juneau side did not know that it had safely returned to Carcross. Newspaper reporters pronounced the Bickell party "lost." A full search party was assembled. A young clerk led prayers for the "missing party" back in Hepburn's Ontario office. Smith's "disappearance" was reported in Auburn, New York's *Citizen-Advertiser* in a piece that read more like an obituary than a missing person's report.[64] The morning papers, however, corrected the misinformation and declared that the mining millionaire and his friends were safe. When the party returned to Ontario on August 7, Hepburn discussed the trip and the political winds with reporters on the veranda of Bickell's Mississauga estate.[65]

The idea of a new political party, if there really had been one, amounted to nothing, especially when the Second World War broke out. Bickell remained engaged with Hepburn during his last years in office. In 1939 Hepburn spent some time with Bickell at his Sea Island estate in Georgia before they embarked on a leisurely cruise in the Caribbean.[66] In 1940 Hepburn was quite ill. On June 26 of that same year, Mitch was carried on a stretcher on board J.P.'s plane. The destination was Kellogg Sanitarium in Battle Creek, Michigan. The short respite helped and Mitch returned to work for a time.[67] During the war, Hepburn hoped to join Bickell in his work with the Ministry of Aircraft Production in England. Reporters queried Bickell in 1941 as to whether or not Hepburn would serve under Lord Beaverbrook, to which J.P. responded: "I don't care to say anything about that until I have had a chance to talk with Mr. Hepburn."[68] Truthfully, although Bickell missed his old friend, he was not prepared to "get in wrong with Bill [Mackenzie] King by doing anything."[69] In other words, J.P. was not prepared to bring Mitch into the fold given the importance of his work in England and knowing the tempestuous relationship Ontario's premier had with Canada's prime minister. Bickell's return missive to Hepburn was simple: best wishes from "one dead drunk to another."[70]

Several keen observers had pegged Mitchell Hepburn as a potential future prime minister of Canada. But many obstacles stood in the way, not least of which was his inability (read: refusal) to work with Prime Minister Mackenzie King. Mitch's proclivity for spending more time with his fast and famous friends may also have halted any possible move from the King Eddy to Laurier House. Mitch lacked, as Saywell concluded, those crucial characteristics such as patience, self-discipline, forward planning and a "talent for semantic ambiguity" that might have otherwise propelled him into the nation's top political position.[71] In the end, J.P. could not rescue his friend from his battle with King and all of King's men. Soon, Bickell became rather less invested in the slight shift in political winds breezing across Canada and far more concerned with the world-altering gusts howling across Europe.

5

War

The Four B's and the Battle of Britain

In the months leading up to the Second World War, Bickell, perhaps in anticipation of the historical events that were about to explode, chose to make a change. At the end of 1938, J.P. decided to leave Thomson and McKinnon. He had been considering the move for months, as the *New York Times* attested:

> Mr. Bickell is known to have desired to leave the brokerage business for some time, and discussed the step as much as a year ago when he took Bernard E. Smith, his intimate for many years, into the firm. Mr. Bickell, it will be recalled, was with Mr. Smith last summer when the broker's plane was forced down in the Yukon territory.[1]

"Sell 'Em Ben" took over the Thomson and McKinnon reins on January 1, 1939.[2] Six months later, the fifty-four-year-old Bickell would undertake what would surely be the most important appointment of his life.

J.P. Bickell's commitment to the war effort is incontestable. The *Star Weekly* would later surmise that during the war, Bickell was likely "the biggest individual sender of food parcels to Britain."[3] While this humanitarian initiative surely counts for much, Bickell's real value in stopping the Nazis took place in the air. At the outset of the war Bickell donated his two amphibious planes to the RCAF, but these were merely token gestures. Ultimately, Bickell's efforts were concentrated on sourcing, building, repairing, and making operational those planes required to thwart Operation Sea Lion: Hitler's plan to invade the United Kingdom. By the time Bickell arrived in England, Britain was the last nation in Europe still standing up to the Nazis. Yet Britain was only just hanging on.

Bickell was recruited by the Ministry of Aircraft Production, led by Max Aitken, who had been made Lord Beaverbrook. Chiefly, Bickell was called in to help speed up the production of aircraft to fight the Luftwaffe in the all-important Battle of Britain in 1940. Aitken was a Canadian financier, politician, and successful newspaper proprietor in Britain. He had made his fortune through the amalgamation of Canada's cement industry. After moving to England in 1910, Aitken bought a majority interest in London's *Daily Express* and later founded the *Sunday Express*. Later still, Aitken acquired London's *Evening Standard* and Glasgow's *Evening Citizen*. The newspaper baron became a real baron, accepting a peerage in 1916. During the First World War, Beaverbrook served in the cabinet as chancellor of the Duchy of Lancaster and minister of information, which made him the man responsible for propaganda in Britain and its allies (especially his home country Canada), as well as in neutral countries. Then after the Second World War broke out, as a good friend of Winston Churchill, Beaverbrook was called upon to lead the Ministry of Aircraft Production. The then sixty-six-year-old Churchill phoned his sixty-one-year-old friend Aitken incessantly over a twenty-four-hour period until the latter finally acquiesced and accepted the position.

Max knew he needed help, and that included help from his friend Jack.[4] Beaverbrook's simple cable stated: "If you will come here and assist me we would welcome you."[5] Before Bickell could help Beaverbrook, however, he first had to get to England, a task that was often difficult in wartime. Bickell travelled by clipper from North America to Lisbon and from there to London. When the plane was only a few hundred miles off Britain's shores, the pilot was ordered back due to the presence of enemy aircraft over England. With not enough gas to make it back to Portugal, the pilot chose to press on, streaking through clouds to keep out of sight.[6] They made it.

Once he arrived in England, Bickell joined a foursome that would soon be known as the Four Busy B's. It was an all-Canadian group of men consisting of Lord Beaverbrook, former Canadian Prime Minister R.B. Bennett, Toronto-born British MP Beverley Baxter, and J.P. Bickell.[7] Beaverbrook chose his aides wisely. According to the *Winnipeg Tribune:*

J.P. Bickell (centre) and Lord Beaverbrook (right) in Nassau, The Bahamas.

[Beaverbrook] took all authority and shared it jealously with men of his choosing, men who knew their jobs and were willing to accept responsibility.... Lord Beaverbrook drives his organization just as he drives himself — at high speed.[8]

Led by Beaverbrook's boundless energy and determination, the Busy B's worked tirelessly to procure the necessary planes for the Allies during the dreadful and dreary days of the Blitz.

Bickell was dearly valued by Beaverbrook, who sought his advice on several issues.[9] Bickell was specifically put in charge of moving aircraft from the factories to the airfields for both training and operations. As Bickell informed Toronto reporters in 1941:

We had to move the aircraft, because if we didn't the enemy would be able to destroy them during air raids on the factories. We started with a very small personnel and our transfer pilots were civilians who were either too old or for physical reasons were unfit for

Lord Beaverbrook (Canadian Max Aitken), minister of aircraft production in Churchill's wartime government and responsible for the Atlantic Ferry Organization (ATFERO).

the R.A.F. We couldn't spare any men from the R.A.F. for this duty as they were needed too much in the battle against the German Luftwaffe. In September of last year, not a fit man could be spared from that. From a small nucleus this organization has grown until last August, when I left England, it was over 1,600 strong and was moving aircraft to safety as fast as they were turned out by the factories.[10]

As part of his responsibilities, Bickell was charged with making sure that damaged planes would be retrieved from squadron bases and taken to the depots so that they might be repaired and returned to service as soon as possible.[11] Bickell was right in the thick of it. When Air Marshal Billy Bishop visited Bickell's Belgrade Square home in London during the Battle of Britain, a bomb crashed just outside the residence, scattering plaster and glass.[12] It was the production of the desperately needed aircraft required to stop the Nazis that earned J.P. and the other B's their well-deserved credibility.

The Air Transport Auxiliary (ATA) in which Bickell worked was commanded by Commander Gerald D'Erlanger. Like Bickell, D'Erlanger had come to England to help Beaverbrook at the Ministry of Aircraft Production. Together, D'Erlanger and Bickell were able to accelerate production in the factories so that the planes could get out to the fighter and bomber stations where they were so urgently needed. Officially, Bickell was the controller of the ATA; he was much admired by his colleagues for the speed in which he got results.[13] Given his high-ranking position, Bickell was privy to many of the Allies' top secrets. Through his connections to the Scottish scientist Robert Watson-Watt, the man responsible for the development of radar, Bickell knew that Britain had had the main installation of radar completed as early as 1937. The Germans wouldn't learn this information until after the Battle of Britain had been decided. Such vital information was shared only with a precious few people. Bickell was among this high-level group.

Circumstances called on Bickell to go back and forth between Canada and Britain. On one occasion, having just completed a two-week trip to Ottawa and Washington on behalf of the British Air Ministry, Bickell was set to return to England from Newfoundland. Before he left Bickell dropped in at the Royal Canadian Air Force Officers' Mess. Spotting a few freshly caught speckled brook trout, Bickell asked one of the officers if he could take some back to England with him. The officer agreed and soon Bickell and his fish were on their way. J.P. arrived in England only minutes from when Canadian Air Minister C.G. Power also touched down. Bickell, according to the *Globe and Mail*, "produced the tin and the cook in the Royal Air Force Officers' Mess prepared a tasty dish, which was shared among the passengers of both aircraft. All the fish disappeared."[14]

Far more importantly, in February 1941 the Busy B's managed to produce a greater number of bombers and fighters than in any single month up until that point in the war. The success was due in part to Beaverbrook's unconventional ways. As Colonel John Jestyn Llewellin opined in March of that year, Beaverbrook's methods "got a move on in the whole aircraft industry which has been completely phenomenal since the time he came into office." The peculiarity of Beaverbrook's ways, Llewellin added, "must be put in the vast perspective behind the man largely responsible for helping to defeat the enemy all last year."[15] Beverley Baxter corroborated Llewellin's findings:

> The House has to accept this extraordinary man with all the difficulties of temperament he undoubtedly possesses to a marked degree. At any given moment Lord Beaverbrook can be proved wrong, but in the end he has a terrific habit of being proved right. I beg the House not to exaggerate the importance of these temperamental difficulties which occur wherever this Minister is in charge.[16]

Beaverbrook's own and indeed the "temperamental difficulties" of the other B's proved to be a huge boon for the Allied cause. This gumption and guile won the admiration of Winston Churchill, who said that through the efforts of the Busy B's the increase in aircraft manufacturing had been "astounding."[17]

Bickell also handled, at least for a time, the Atlantic Ferry Organization or ATFERO, the chief responsibility of which was to ferry aircraft from the Canadian Pacific Air Services to Britain. Bickell ran ATFERO from the British side during the first half of 1941, and his good work made news back home.[18] In *The Caduceus*, the staff magazine of the Canadian Bank of Commerce, Bickell was lauded for his new position:

> The Bank can indeed feel justifiably proud of the service being rendered to the nation and the Empire by Mr. MacMillan [who had been appointed Chairman of the Wartime Requirements Board] and by his fellow Directors, Mr. J.P. Bickell, who has joined Lord Beaverbrook's Ministry for Aircraft Production, and Mr. George R. Cottrelle, Oil Controller for Canada.[19]

Cottrelle, it will be recalled, was also an executive member of the Maple Leaf Gardens Board of Directors. During this same period, Bickell's friend Sydney Logan was appointed a committee member representing the Secretary of State for the British Air Ministry. It seemed that all of Bickell's pals were rolling up their sleeves to get the job done.

Bickell was exceeding expectations. He was, as one *Toronto Star* headline exclaimed, doing an "impossible job" for the war effort.[20] Captain Norman Edgar, director of the Auxiliary Air Transport Service of Britain, was particularly pleased with Bickell's resolve and resources:

> [Bickell has done] one of the really fine jobs of the war. In a year under his leadership, the auxiliary

air transport service has been expanded 500 per cent.… He has built up one of the largest and smoothest-working civilian organizations in the history of warfare. He has been in control of all ferrying and delivering of planes in the United Kingdom.[21]

Yet in his work ferrying bombers across the Atlantic for the RAF Bickell was perhaps even more effective. Edgar explained that by cutting through red tape and "by direct action and amazing drive and organizing ability, Mr. Bickell has done a work which appeared impossible to accomplish within the time it has been effective."[22] Bickell was a key reason that the transatlantic plane ferry service became functional. Lord Beaverbrook himself told reporters that "Jack Bickell thinks red tape is something that should be thrown into the waste-paper basket.… He gets things done and he gets them done quickly."[23] How quickly Britain needed those planes to keep Hitler on the other side of the Channel!

Bickell the Bomber

Beaverbrook and Bickell were in Washington in the summer of 1941 to obtain more weapons and foodstuffs from the Americans, who were still a few months from joining the war.[24] Following this meeting Bickell returned to Canada with Beaverbrook. The latter was on his way to the famous Atlantic Charter Conference off the coast of Ship Harbour, Newfoundland, on August 14. With Roosevelt and the Americans now taking a more muscular stand against Hitler, and given the resolve that the British had demonstrated during the Blitz, Bickell told reporters that he was more optimistic as to the outcome of the war: "I think things are looking more encouraging all the time."[25]

On reflection, Bickell, who had personally borne witness to the horrors of the Blitz, saw the British people — a people he already admired so deeply — during their finest hour:

There is no doubt but that we have won the first battle, the battle for survival. And I am certain that we will win the second one, that for victory, although I cannot tell how long it may be before that is gained. It may be a long, hard, struggle, but we will win in the end. Today our armies are well equipped and there is no intention of just blundering through. It is altogether different from slightly over a year ago, just after Dunkirk. Our losses in material and equipment there were enormous and we were lucky that Jerry didn't follow up his advantage then. If he had, we would have had to fight the invaders with pitchforks and stones. Everything that was lost there has been replaced with better materials and equipment, and we have lots more. Our position is such that we have every confidence in the final result.[26]

When pressed on specifics as they related to his duties, Bickell kept his descriptions vague, telling those who had assembled to meet him in Toronto: "You might say that I have finished the work I was doing. I think that is the best way to put it."[27] As it happened, Bickell's war work was far from finished.

In 1942 Bickell cut a cheque for five thousand dollars, which he donated to the RCAF's Benevolent Fund. In a letter that accompanied the cheque, Bickell wrote with warmth and deliberation of his feelings for the RCAF's fighting men and their contribution to the war effort:

If there is any branch of the services which merits recognition in a deferential degree, surely it must be that in which the personnel suffer the highest percentage of casualties in relationship to their numbers, namely the air force. Furthermore, I am firmly convinced that had it not been for the indomitable courage, skill and sacrifices endured by them during the Battle of Britain, the destiny of democracy everywhere would long since have been shattered beyond recognition, if not completely eliminated. When one realizes that the age range in this group comprises mainly of those just on the threshold of life and normally therefore with the longest expectancy before them, the tragedy to both them and their families becomes even more poignant.[28]

Bickell's gift was, according to him, but a tiny symbol of his respect, admiration and esteem for the men of the air force and their "immortal deeds."[29]

Bickell's own immortal deeds were not yet complete. His return to Canada in 1942 did not signal an end to his toiling on behalf of the Allied cause. Central to the British Air Ministry's operations — and indeed the war effort — was the government-owned Victory Aircraft in Malton.[30] Vitally, Victory Aircraft, with Bickell as president, manufactured Lancaster bombers for the air war against the Nazis. At the end of July 1943 the *Financial Post* confirmed:

The Ruhr Express *over the Victory Aircraft plant in Malton, Ontario. Illustration by Michael Martchenko.*

Canadian-made Lancaster bombers will soon start coming from the assembly lines of Victory Aircraft, Malton, Ont. Head of the Crown company producing the bomber is James [*sic*] Paris Bickell, Ontario mining millionaire, who served with Lord Beaverbrook when the latter was Minister of Aircraft Production in England. Like Churchill, Bickell is famous for his preference for cigars.[31]

J.P., puffing away on his trademark cigar, went about the crucial business of pushing out as many Lancaster bombers as possible. In short order, the "Lanc" would become the most important bomber used during the war. In over 156,000 sorties, the Lancaster delivered 618,378 tonnes of bombs.[32]

The Lancaster was central to Air Chief Marshal Arthur "Bomber" Harris's Operation Gomorrah in July 1943. The now controversial result was the utter destruction of Hamburg.[33] The bomber was

Air Marshal H. Edwards of the RCAF (third from left) with the "Bluenose" bomber group in England. He is escorting J.P. Bickell (second from right), president, and R.P. Bell (fourth from left), director of aircraft production, Victory Aircraft, October 19, 1943.

J.P. Bickell as guest of Sir Charles Craven, chairman of the Air Supply Board, at the Victory Parade, London, England, June 8, 1946. They both wave hats in the front row. Bickell is on the left.

also used in Operation Chastise, which destroyed the dams along the Ruhr Valley (and later supplied the story to the 1955 movie starring Michael Redgrave and Richard Todd, *The Dam Busters*).[34] In Operation Manna, the Lancaster dropped much-needed food to those who were starving in occupied Netherlands. The bomber was, according to the Commander of the Luftwaffe's fighters Adolf Galland, "the best night bomber of the war."[35] For Air Chief Marshal Harris, the Lancaster was the "shining sword" of the RAF's Bomber Command.[36] In the end, the Lancaster bomber was one of the most important weapons that brought the war to a successful issue for the Allies. J.P. Bickell played an essential part in the forging of Bomber Command's "shining sword."

The End of the Beginning — Victory Aircraft

In late 1943 political machinations caused Bickell to reconsider his position at Victory. When he had taken on the job, Bickell was assured that he would have free rein to bring his own hand-selected team of directors into the Victory Aircraft fold. Governmental powers in Ottawa, however, had different ideas. Ottawa insisted that Bickell add another director to those he had already chosen. It was not that the government had not been happy. On the contrary, C.D. Howe, then minister of munitions and supply, declared that Bickell and his team had been entirely satisfactory in producing Lancasters. It was a team that served, as Bickell did, without salary or expenses.

While Howe may have been pleased with Bickell's output, he had suspicions about the man's openness to certain political perspectives. These suspicions were aroused when Bickell and his board resigned instead of bowing to the demand to have a representative of labour added to it. Bickell explained why he and the board felt that resignation was necessary in a letter to Howe on October 21, 1943:

> It was with certain stipulations and upon a very definite undertaking that I would be permitted to choose my own board of directors. More than that, the final acceptance of my co-directors was predicated on the same undertaking. If then, acquiescence with your suggestion of Sept. 29 is a necessity, it violates our basic understanding. The suggestion that has thus developed has been carefully and earnestly studied by the board members and, not without a measure of regret, we have finally concluded that we should make way for others who can better harmonize their action with Government policy as annunciated from time to time.[37]

Howe did not mince his words in his reply in advance of Bickell's resignation at the end of October 1943:

> It will of course be necessary to give Parliament a reason for such resignations as may take place and to table the correspondence. I presume you and the

members of your board will have no hesitation in publicizing the fact that all members of the board resigned because of government policy adding a representative of organized labour to the board of Victory Aircraft Ltd.[38]

While Howe believed Bickell and company to be jumping ship because a labour representative was being added to their board, Bickell was keen to explain otherwise in his reply of November 26, 1943:

> Once again I must endeavour to make perfectly clear to you that I have not objected … to the adding to the board of a director of a status you require, nor have I even commented on this aspect of the question…. Your demand was made without even conferring with me or giving the directors an opportunity to consider the matter, which course, I think, would have been only fair and reasonable and in keeping with ordinary business ethics, and particularly in this case do I believe this was desirable when it is considered that the members of the board are not Government employees, but independent executives of high standing.[39]

In some ways, Bickell had been caught in the middle of Hepburn's ongoing feud with Mackenzie King. As one of Hepburn's "millionaire friends," Bickell was cast as an enemy of labour, a characterization that had plagued Hepburn for years. It certainly did not help that Bickell and team chose to resign en masse when the director that Ottawa suggested was a labour representative.[40] When pushed to fall in line with government policy, Bickell, along with E.C. Cox, W.K. Fraser, J.J. Vaughan, and J.P.'s good friend Sydney Logan, chose to walk instead.

In fairness, Howe was still extremely complimentary toward Bickell in his letters to the other directors, including one to J.J. Vaughan on January 25, 1944:

> I agree wholly that the Victory Aircraft plant is now on the way to successful operation. I also agree that Mr. Bickell has carried out his responsibilities in a highly efficient manner. No one regrets more than I do that he finds it necessary to retire as president.[41]

Bickell's reputation was impeccable, but he simply wasn't going to play the game by Ottawa rules. His relationship with and feelings about government were fairly clear to those who knew him. As the *Northern Miner* stated:

> When political influence intruded itself [Bickell] withdrew, and his associates went with him, of course. He would agree with a Socialist that governments could operate businesses as well as private people could, but commented that they never did.[42]

While Bickell had obviously taken umbrage with Ottawa over the machinations behind the scenes of Victory Aircraft, he was also quite concerned with the federal government's sheepish policies regarding mining. For a decade leading up to the war, the Canadian government had begun to reconsider its policy on prospecting and development in the mining industry. Bickell believed — and he was not alone in this opinion —— that the feds' fiscal policy had virtually paralyzed the prospector's hand in the mining game, and that a future of diminishing returns could be expected if the government did not reverse its mining strategies.

Robert Laurier, Ontario's minister of mines for a period during the war, was completely on board with Bickell's assessment.

Laurier, who was the nephew of Sir Wilfrid Laurier, called on the federal government and the other metal-producing provinces to come together to find a policy that could correct what was considered by those in the industry to be a grave situation.[43] Bickell's opinion was sacrosanct within the mining community and his warnings did not go unheeded, as the *Globe and Mail's* financial editor Wellington Jeffers observed:

> If something comes of it, many communities across Canada will owe a lot to John P. Bickell for the frank and uncompromising language in which he stated his convictions, and for the quickness and decisiveness with which Ontario's Minister of Mines has taken action. Obviously he is right in suggesting that this saving of the industry is a matter for all Governments. J.P. Bickell has an international record for getting down to earth on all business and public questions. His success in the mining and other ventures in which he hazarded his capital owes as much to his horse sense and his ability to go right to the core of any questions presented to him as to any other factor. His friends and acquaintances know that he has always backed to the limit his underlying faith in the possibilities of development of the mineral resources of the Dominion, and has taken both the rewards and the inevitable losses that belong to such enterprises with equal equanimity. It does not need a long acquaintance with him to realize that his remarks … are not motivated by concern about his own personal interests. He has spoken out, just as he says, because the time has come when those who know the facts should no longer stay silent and let this sad fiscal situation remain as a detriment to future mining

development. He is right in his view that it is a duty
to speak out, no matter what interpretation some
politicians may choose to place on the matter.[44]

Bickell had adroitly observed that by the 1940s, over half of
the country's mining output was produced in areas that had been
discovered prior to 1910, and that approximately 95 percent
was being produced in areas discovered prior to 1930, which
suggested that no significant mining development had occurred
in Canada in the previous fifteen years. Ergo, mining was a
wasting asset.

Bickell's principal issue was that Canada's future developers
and prospectors were not being encouraged by the government.
Indeed, new policies dissuaded many would-be developers and
prospectors, who were put off by the knowledge that they would
forgo, through red tape and taxation, much of what they might
find should they actually get lucky in the first place. These policies
restricted the dreams of a life in precious metals for many people.

In 1945 the Ontario Securities Act further tightened its regulations, discouraging small dealers from embarking on prospec-
tive development. The government's rationale was that the Act
protected the public, but many in the mining industry believed
that this was effectively a charade. In the six years following
the implementation of the revamped Ontario Securities Act, the
number of broker-dealers in the province had dropped from several hundred to a paltry eighty. As the *Globe and Mail* reported
in October 1951, only months after Bickell had died, under the
new regulations honest brokers were being forced out of business because they could not make a decent wage, while dishonest
men were attracted to mining because they could make a profit
through unlawful means: "It was parallel to the situation under
the Ontario Temperance Act, where the tighter the regulations
against drinking became the more bootleggers there were."[45]
Thomas A. Sutton, chairman of the American Stockholders'

Union, testified at Queen's Park in Toronto that the present regulations deprived Canadians of their birthright and of free enterprise as mining development was increasingly falling into the hands of monopoly capitalism. Sutton also pointed out, with perhaps a touch of levity:

> If we'd had these regulations in the days of (Sir) Harry Oakes and Mr. Bickell … they wouldn't have wound up as heads of mining companies. They would have wound up in jail.[46]

Though J.P. Bickell had left the planet by the time Sutton made his point, he continued even in death to serve as a Cassandra looking darkly into the future. And the warning remained the same as it had been during the last decade of the man's life: relax the restrictive policies and give future dreamers the same shot J.P. Bickell had.

A.V. Roe Canada Limited

The woes of the mining industry were only one of the many issues plaguing Bickell in his later years. Out of the war's ashes, and following his controversial departure from Victory, Bickell was to co-found and become chairman of A.V. Roe Canada Limited in 1945. J.P. put up the bulk of the money himself. This was at a time when the North American aircraft industry had virtually collapsed.

Avro's team was led by its president, Sir Roy Dobson, who named the company after his own existing aircraft company back in England: A.V. Roe Ltd., Manchester. The English version had been the world's largest and most versatile company of its kind. Dobson was flanked by Walter N. Deisher, the Malton plant's general manager and, of course, Bickell, who was the aircraft company's chairman of the board, a position he held until his death.[47]

J.P. Bickell, Sir Archibald Rowlands, and Sir Roy Dobson at the RAF At Home Day celebration commemorating the Battle of Britain, September 16, 1950.

J.P. Bickell (left) enjoying a game of dominoes with Sir Roy Dobson (centre) and a friend aboard the RMS Queen Elizabeth.

Although it was run by Canadians, A.V Roe Canada was never-theless a subsidiary of the British Hawker Siddeley Group, set up in 1945 on a bank draft personally guaranteed by Jack Bickell.[48] Commonly known as Avro, like its British parent, the company was incorporated on September 1, 1945, with a capital stock of $2.5 million (250,000 shares at par value).[49] The opening of the Canadian factory was heralded within the airplane industry. *Flight* magazine, for instance, reported:

> A.V. Roe and Co., Ltd., have purchased from the Canadian Government the Malton, Ontario plant of Victory Aircraft, Ltd., established during the war to build Lancasters.... The formation of the entirely reorganized company's board has not yet been com-pleted, but Sir Roy Dobson is to be its president, Mr. J.P. Bickell, the Canadian who was entrusted with the formation of Atfero early in the war, will be chairman.[50]

The staff at A.V. Roe set about trying to prove its worth as a Canadian company in an industry dominated by the British and the Americans. This included the Jetliner development. The idea of passengers paying to fly on a jet airplane was, of course, a novel idea at this time, and even some war-hardened pilots simply could not fathom it. Still, some people could. Bickell numbered among the visionaries. On August 10, 1949, A.V. Roe put its Jetliner, North America's first jet passenger aircraft, in the air. Though it flew mostly test flights for much of its short existence, it must be recalled that the company's Jetliner predated Boeing's 707 by a full five years.[51] And even though he had passed away before A.V. Roe set its designs on the famous Avro Arrow, Bickell's significant investment in the company was proven to be a worthy one.[52]

Avro Aircraft advertisement, including a photo of a CF 100 flying over the Victory Aircraft plant in Malton, Ontario.

A.V. Roe Canada Company personnel including Chairman Bickell (centre, in top hat), and guests attending the official flight of the Jetliner, October 4, 1949.

A.V. Roe officials watching the flight of the Avro Jetliner at Malton, Ontario, October 4, 1949. Bickell is fourth from the right.

Walter Deisher (centre left), vice-president and general manager of A.V. Roe Canada, and J.P. Bickell (centre right), chairman, standing in front of the Jetliner's engines.

Standards

Regardless of how many pokers Bickell may have had in the fire, his name was still synonymous with mining. At the war's end, Bickell wanted to ease the anxiety of the general public. In short, he wanted everyone to know that it would soon be business as usual at McIntyre Porcupine. At the company's annual meeting in 1945, only weeks after Germany surrendered, Bickell declared:

> The producing mines such as our own have large underground development programs ready for immediate application. Increased daily capacity will come naturally as this work proceeds.[53]

Bickell was hoping to assuage fears about the mining industry in general. Perhaps not surprisingly, McIntyre Porcupine had had an unusually slow time in that last year of the war. At fiscal year end, March 31, 1945, McIntyre Porcupine reported a net profit of $2,355,807. That was down approximately $500,000 from the previous year. Accordingly, bullion production was also down from the previous year. The tonnage mined and milled was, as the *Toronto Star* reported on May 30, 1945, "curtailed, the gross value of production decreased and unit costs maintained an upward trend."[54] Yet perhaps the trend that most worried Bickell was the international push to come off of the gold standard in the years following the war.

The hotly contested debate surrounding the gold standard had raged for nearly a century. At issue was the question of whether or not countries should still base their money supply on the size of their stores of gold. The debate became particularly heated during the leanest years of the Depression. Bickell, not surprisingly, was a champion of the gold standard, as he explained:

> The eternal quality of its indestructibility imparts a security in perpetuity for which mankind is ever seeking. Until such a time as some other form of money which cannot be debased is found, or until the pledge of both governments and individuals can be accepted as inviolate under all conditions, gold will become as it has in the past, progressively more valuable in terms of promises to pay.[55]

This letter of Bickell's was later reread by proponents of the gold standard in the American Senate in 1954, three years after Bickell's death.

William Henry Moore, a lawyer, economist, and Liberal MP for the riding of Ontario, was also a staunch proponent of gold. In *Yellow Metal*, a book he dedicated to his friend J.P. Bickell, Moore explained:

If we had succeeded in our efforts to replace monetary gold by "something else" in which people had equal confidence, then, the nations would not have been compelled to reduce the buying powers of their units of currency and more gold would not now be essential. Having attempted to devise substitutes, and having failed to secure something "just as good," we are now not likely to succeed while the world is covered with distrust. And so in the turn of events, Canada is called upon to make a contribution to world recovery. For my part I can think of no greater contribution than to tell the world that Canada will restore prosperity on the stage of Economic Liberalism. Prosperity has the temperament of a prima donna, but with all her faults let us bring her back.[56]

For his part, J.P. publicly criticized the theorists he thought were simply incorrect:

Each new scheme but adds to the general confusion, and the greater the confusion becomes the more urgent and insistent will the demand finally become for a return to that standard which served us so well and is known and understood not only by the financial experts but by mankind in practically every country and all walks of life.[57]

Bickell took advantage of several opportunities to vociferously warn those who championed artificial currencies, as the *Northern Miner* explained:

"J.P." believed that government management and control of money and production could result in gross

mismanagement, so when he was operating government enterprises he insisted that business methods
take precedence over the theories of government
advisers. He could appreciate political considerations
but felt that they would only be served, in a crown
corporation, by the best of direction.[58]

Alas, while Bickell may have been railing against the Keynesian
theorists about the future of the gold standard, and in some cases
with success, the system's days were numbered. Today, no country
in the world uses it as the basis of its monetary system. Investment
in gold in the recent past is likewise down, which has been, as
the *Globe and Mail*'s David Berman observed in 2014, "reflected
in the price: It has fallen to about $1,320 (U.S.) an ounce, down
$580 or more than forty percent from its record high in 2011."[59]
Indeed, gold suffered an annual decline in 2013 that would be
its worst in over three decades.

Solace

In the 1940s, however, the centrality of gold to J.P.'s grand narrative remained firm. Bickell and his empire were a celebrated
Canadian story. While he may have been a young, upstart millionaire from humble origins in the 1910s, he had now, as a man
in his early sixties, become a perennial member of Canada's who's
who. Bickell figured several times in *Who Owns Canada?*, a book
by Watt Hugh McCollum that listed and rated the country's biggest movers and shakers in 1947. Bickell cracked McCollum's list
of "Canada's Fifty 'Big Shots.'"[60]
    Despite his guarded private life and his reluctance to spend
too much time in the media's spotlight, Bickell really was a
certifiable Big Shot. He continued to serve, as he had done
for years, on many boards, both philanthropic and otherwise.

Bickell served as a director of the Health League of Canada, and was also a director on the board for the St. John Ambulance Association.[61] In 1948 Bickell was also vice-president of the Canadian Metal Mining Association.[62] The association was unique in the mining industry and worked on far-ranging initiatives such as bringing specially screened immigrants to work the mines, the first 1,400 of which were ready to arrive at the end of 1948. The workers were, according to the *Globe and Mail*, "willing, hard and able workers, giving every promise of establishing themselves as useful Canadians."[63]

Nearing the time of his death, Bickell remained chairman of McIntyre Porcupine, Castle Trethewey, Belleterre Quebec, and A.V. Roe Canada. He was, until the end, a director for the Canadian Bank of Commerce, Imperial Life Assurance, National Trust Company, St. Mary's Cement Company, and International Nickel Company of Canada (INCO).

J.P. was not all work and no play, and was certainly not a dull boy. He had kept up his membership at the Royal Canadian Yacht Club and the Mississaugua Golf and Country Club, and he was also a member of the Toronto Hunt Club, the infamous San Francisco Bohemian Club, the Surf Club at Miami Beach, the Albany, the Chicago Athletic Club, and the York Club in downtown Toronto. Yet, perhaps as a combination of his work and philanthropic commitments, not to mention his love of life in the fast lane, the stout captain of gold was being stretched a little thin. Much as he tried, in the last weeks of his life Bickell was not strong enough to continue his normal (and for some, impossible) lifestyle.

Nearing the end of his days, he found more solace at his good friend Sydney Logan's serene Shanty Bay residence than he did at his own Hollywood-esque estate in Mississauga.[64] Perhaps sensing that his time was coming to an end, he wanted to see his friend "Logie." Bickell called the Logans and got Hilda on the line. As daughter Anne recollected:

[J.P. asked,] "Have you got a lot of company this weekend?" Mom said "no." "Would you mind if I flew up for the weekend?" And mom said, "We'd love to have a visit from you." And that visit was the last time they saw him. It was as if [J.P.] knew.

In only a matter of weeks J.P. would be dead.

In late July 1951 Bickell suffered a slight stroke. Undeterred, he moved on and was resolute, choosing to ignore the warning signs, as the *Northern Miner* explained: "in characteristic disdain of difficulty or disability, he brushed them aside, said they would pass away, and continued on with his intensely active business life."[65] A little more than three weeks after his stroke Bickell travelled to New York. He was hospitalized almost immediately upon arrival, entering the New York Hospital in Manhattan on August 17.

Just over a month shy of his sixty-seventh birthday, John Paris Bickell died on Thursday, August 22, 1951.[66]

If there was any comfort during the time of his passing it was that his good friend Ben Smith was there at his side. Coincidentally, Ben's son Jim and his wife were at the hospital at the same time expecting the birth of their first child, which occurred on August 18, just four days before Jack's passing. Jack loved children and it would have made him happy knowing his good friend Ben was a new grandpa.

Benevolence

Bickell the Benevolent

J.P. Bickell's funeral was held on August 25, with the interment in Toronto's Mount Pleasant Mausoleum.[1] Predictably, there was an outpouring of condolences. The Director's Report in the Canadian Bank of Commerce's *Annual Report* lamented:

> It is with deep sorrow and a sense of personal loss that we record the death last August of Mr. John Paris Bickell. Mr. Bickell was elected a member of the Board in April 1928 and over the long period since that date, by his valuable services as a Director, contributed greatly to the growth and progress of the Bank.[2]

Similarly, the Board of Directors at the National Trust Company offered:

> As a Director of this Company and deeply interested in its welfare, Mr. Bickell will be greatly missed by

his fellow-members of the Board and by the executive officers of the Company to whom his advice and experienced counsel were always freely available.[3]

Beyond the institutions, almost every major newspaper in Canada paid tribute to the recently deceased champion of the mining industry.

While he was alive, Bickell was quite likely the largest personal taxpayer in Canada.[4] Indeed, Bickell felt a deep sense of duty to his nation and had contempt for those wealthy Canadians who left Canada to escape taxation.[5] When he died, Bickell's estate was worth over $14.5 million.[6] The numbers broke down as follows: the estate was worth $12,379,155; bonds and stocks totalled $1,603,350; insurance was $455,000; household goods and motor cars added up to $95,747; and Bickell's miscellaneous assets counted for $44,265.[7] Excepting a few small bequests to some of his employees, associates, and the Art Gallery of Ontario, and one to his sister, Marjorie Paulin, the bulk of J.P.'s money — some $13 million — went to philanthropy, specifically the charitable organization called the J.P. Bickell Foundation. By 2010's standards, Bickell's $13 million donation would actually be closer to a staggering $120 million.

Apart from the Foundation, Bickell looked after his nearest and dearest. J.P.'s sister and only surviving sibling, Marjorie, was the Bickells' youngest child, born on November 4, 1890. Marjorie married the Reverend Dr. James B. Paulin in 1936. A First World War veteran, Paulin was the minister of Toronto's Rosedale Presbyterian Church (1918–24, 1934–49) and for a time served as the reverend at St. Andrew's College (1931–32), St. Paul's Presbyterian Church, and St. Giles Presbyterian Church in Hamilton. Marjorie Paulin, like her brother J.P., was an avid golfer and belonged to both the Mississaugua and Toronto Ladies' golf clubs. (J.P. loaned Ada McKenzie the remaining $8,000 two hours before her deadline to found the Ladies Golf Club of Toronto. As Ada McKenzie explained, "It was Mr. Bickell who saved our life."[8]) Also like her brother, Marjorie was a Leafs fan; she presented the first J.P. Bickell Memorial Award to the team's captain, Ted Kennedy, in 1953. No doubt inspired by her brother's various initiatives, Marjorie gave generously toward scholarships and bursaries for mining students, specifically through the Women's Association of the Mining Industry in Canada.[9] J.P. left Marjorie all of his jewellery, his sterling silver, his plate and plated articles, linen, china, and books. He also left her $100,000 and a yearly sum of $2,400 to be paid out of the proposed J.P. Bickell Foundation — by this time her husband had retired from the ministry.

Bickell also paid his associates and staffers a kind tribute out of his will. J.P.'s secretary Kelley Butler received $10,000, as did employees E.D. Fox and William B. Dix. Bickell's chauffeur Charles Harrod likewise received $10,000. Frank Blount, J.P.'s chef, was given $2,000, while his housekeeper Ethel Waldick received $1,000 plus an annuity of $1,200 per annum.[10] Thoughtfully, if somewhat less extravagantly, J.P. left his snares in the Hillsburgh Fishing Club to Balmer Neilly, his successor as president of McIntyre Porcupine, who also served on the University of Toronto board of governors.

The largest bequest Bickell made, however, went to his now very famous foundation. The organization's chief aim was to affect positive change in the medical and educational fields, and, wherever possible, to assist existing like-minded charitable organizations in Ontario. Bickell's foundation limited its payments to charities within the province because of the Ontario Succession Duty Act, which exempted only those charitable organizations operating within Ontario from succession duties. In the case of Bickell's bequest these would have been significant and would have therefore reduced the benefits paid out.

J.P. gave specific instructions as to how the Foundation's money was to be distributed. Ten percent of the income was intended for charitable or educational organizations in Ontario for medical research. Five percent was to be used in developing or establishing scholarships and/or bursaries in the mining industry, which included geological and geophysical fields. Thirty-five percent of the Foundation's income was to be disbursed at the discretion of the trustees to various organizations in Ontario. Bickell explained his reasoning in his last will and testament:

> Realizing that it would be injudicious and egotistical for any individual to attempt to forecast future conditions even for a decade after his death, and believing that the most effective way of devoting to the public welfare a substantial part of the assets which I have accumulated during my lifetime is to rely on the integrity, experience and judgment of those who, in my opinion, will be in the best position to judge and select those charitable and worthy objects most deserving of support from time to time in the light of then current conditions, I have resolved to leave to the discretion of my Trustees, within certain limits, the selection of such charitable objects.[11]

The lion's share of income generated by the J.P. Bickell Foundation was earmarked for Toronto's Hospital for Sick Children. The arrangement for this subsidy, precisely half of the annual net income of the Foundation, was made in perpetuity.[12]

It must be recalled that these were still the early days of the Cold War, and Bickell's gift gave some the opportunity to champion the free market system. The *Ottawa Journal*, for instance, declared:

> J.P. Bickell's money is passed on into channels in which it can accomplish tremendous things in the relief of suffering and in the advancement of human well-being. Such events redound to the glory of the

men who engage in them, and they are only possible under the free enterprise system. The keen personal incentive which they stimulate, in a hospital,
say, is much preferable to the pallid pedestrianism of
the socialization being so loudly preached by dema-
gogues these days.[13]

Though such editorializing might have pleased "Smiling Jack,"
championing the free market system was not the impetus that
pushed him to help those who were in need.

Indeed, Bickell's campaign to ameliorate the conditions of
others did not begin with his foundation. In life, and perhaps
inspired by the events surrounding his siblings during his childhood, Bickell had always sought to improve the lives of people
— and especially children — who were suffering. During the
Second World War, for instance, Bickell personally sponsored
and supported a hundred young British children who had come
to Canada.[14] This was only one example of the many actions J.P.
took to benefit those in need.

Bickell had also played an important role in the movement
to make the pasteurization of milk mandatory in Ontario. His
good pal Premier Mitchell Hepburn had become particularly
engaged with the issue of poliomyelitis. In the late summer
of 1937 there was a serious outbreak of polio across Ontario.
Over 2,200 people contracted the disease in Toronto alone. The
epidemic weighed heavily on hospitals that were taxed beyond
their capacity. Hepburn brought Bickell into the conversation
about polio prevention and also new methods of treatment.
Dr. John L. McDonald invited Bickell to visit the Hospital for
Sick Children to observe the iron lungs that were in operation
there. J.P. was profoundly moved at the sight of the machines
but was also moved by those children suffering from bovine
tuberculosis. Bickell wanted Hepburn to see what he had seen.

The following week Bickell threw a dinner party, inviting the premier and Doctors D.E. Robertson, Alan Brown, and John McDonald. The evening included a trip to the Hospital for Sick Children, where Bickell, Hepburn, and company visited the infectious ward. Here they saw four small children breathing comfortably with their iron lungs. In addition to this, Hepburn was able to witness the dreadful effects of bovine tuberculosis, as well as the treatments that were being employed to counter the disease. Having borne witness to the young children, necks bandaged from surgery that removed tuberculous glands, Hepburn was, according to G.C. Brink, director of the Division of Tuberculosis Prevention, "deeply impressed and emotionally disturbed by what he had seen."[15]

Toronto, for its part, had passed a by-law that required the pasteurization of all milk sold in the city. The result was that no child born and raised in Toronto had been admitted to the Hospital for Sick Children suffering from bovine tuberculosis. All children who had been admitted because of the disease had come to the hospital from homes outside of Toronto. As far as Hepburn was concerned it was a clear-cut case: children should not have to suffer from bovine tuberculosis if it could be prevented, and pasteurization of milk promised to eliminate this disease in children.

In a matter of weeks, Hepburn, with the help of doctors Robertson, Brown, and K.G. Gray, who had prepared the legislation, was able to take the proposed bill to the Liberal caucus. As Brink recorded:

> During the discussion of the Bill in caucus, a member rose from his chair and walked in front of the assembled group. He was a cripple with a hunched back, the result of tuberculosis of the spine. Facing the group he said: "Gentlemen, if you have any doubts about the wisdom of this bill, look at me. I am a victim of dirty milk."[16]

The effect was dramatic and the bill passed without a single dissenting voice. Hepburn's crusade against "dirty milk" had been, at least in part, put into motion on the initiative of his friend J.P. Bickell.

J.P.'s role in confronting conditions related to the lungs was not limited to bovine tuberculosis. McIntyre Porcupine was among the world leaders in addressing the frightful issue of silicosis, an occupational lung disease caused by inhalation of crystalline silica dust. This type of pneumoconiosis was all too common in the mines and haunted the minds of many miners. Together, Sir Frederick Banting and J.P. Bickell guided an examination of the effects of silicosis. The initiative also began to develop potential cures, preventative and otherwise.[17] Specifically, the Banting Institute sought to eliminate, or at least reduce, the solubility of silica particles. To do so, small quantities of metallic aluminum dust were used in a two-stage dry, which miners would pass through on their return to the surface. This treatment, the so-called aluminum prophylaxis (or aluminum therapy) was developed at McIntyre by the mine's own physician Dr. W.D. Robson and engineer J.J. Denny. According to the *Star Weekly*, Bickell "footed a tremendous bill for the investigations that proved aluminum dust [was] a preventative."[18]

The initiative hastened the formation of McIntyre Research Limited in 1939. This same organization was, by 1946, known as the McIntyre Research Foundation. Initially, the foundation was formed to further develop and disseminate the process of aluminum prophylaxis throughout the international mining community. It was a process that lasted until 1979, when doctors began to consider aluminum's association with Alzheimer's disease. Yet the foundation's work transcended initiatives aimed at exclusively eradicating silicosis. The non-profit corporation also sought more generally to carry on research and investigation in connection with the prevention, mitigation, and eradication of industrial diseases.[19]

Bickell was also deeply invested in elevating the standards in hospitals and research institutions. Wellesley Hospital was, according to Sydney Logan's daughter Anne, Bickell's most important charity.[20] When Wellesley merged with Toronto General in 1948, J.P. was elected its president. Yet Bickell's interest in public health was not limited to Wellesley Hospital. He sat on the board of governors for both the Canadian Social Hygiene Council and St. John Ambulance.[21] Bickell was constantly giving to the smaller organizations as well, including those in the Timmins area. The *Porcupine Advance*, for example, reported in 1918:

> The members of the Schumacher Red Cross are very pleased with the handsome gift, and the kindly thought prompting the gift recently made to the Society by Mr. J.P. Bickell, president of the McIntyre Porcupine Mines. The gift is a handsome and up-to-date knitting machine. This knitting machine is one of the latest types and the best of its kind. It arrived here this week and will be set up ready for use at the regular meeting of the Schumacher Red Cross Society tomorrow.[22]

Bickell also personally gave — and gave generously — to the Banting Institute for Cancer Research.[23]

Foundation

While many were the recipients of Jack Bickell's kindness while he walked the earth, it was the J.P. Bickell Foundation, established immediately after he died, that has served as his most important and enduring gift. This gift has touched, and continues to touch, countless families. Bickell's gift, among other things, helped to create the Hospital for Sick Children Research Institute in 1954.

The institute is now the largest hospital-based research facility in Canada and one of the largest in the world. Today, nearly a thousand researchers and some of the world's top scientists continue to carry out research there in a variety of medical fields.[24] As a direct result of this work, researchers have located the gene that plays a crucial role in the development of rhabdomyosarcoma (the most common childhood soft tissue cancer). Likewise, doctors at the Hospital for Sick Children successfully performed a lifesaving heart intervention on a baby in utero, which was a Canadian first. Similarly, for the first time in the world they were able to perform an innovative operation using an external artificial lung to keep a pediatric patient alive until new donor lungs became available.[25] It is reasonable to assume that even the great dream-maker himself might not have imagined the overwhelming results of his gracious donation.

In its first two years of operation, the J.P. Bickell Foundation assisted sixty-three charitable and educational organizations. In the organization's first report prepared by the National Trust Company in 1953, the Foundation's trustees declared that $1,013,500 had been distributed since J.P.'s death two years earlier. Leading the pack was, of course, the Hospital for Sick Children, which had received $240,500 in 1952 and $266,250 in 1953. A host of other diverse organizations also received help from the Foundation. Grants were issued to, among others: Frontier College, St. John Ambulance, Boy Scouts Association, St. Faith's Lodge, National Sanatorium Association, John Howard Society of Ontario, Variety Club: Tent 28, Salvation Army, Ontario Society for Crippled Children, Toronto Humane Society, Toronto General Hospital, Huron College, Victorian Order of Nurses, Federation of Ontario Naturalists, Royal Museum of Archaeology, First United Church Port Credit, Society for Crippled Civilians, Toronto's Community Service Fund, Canadian National Institute for the Blind, Home for Incurable Children, Canadian Red Cross Society Ontario

Branch, Scott Mission, and the then-fledgling Stratford Shakespearean Festival of Canada.

At that time, the Stratford Festival was in desperate need of a permanent theatre to solidify itself as the world-class Shakespearean festival it is known as today. The J.P. Bickell Foundation's gift of $100,000 allowed the festival to do just that. The money covered the cost of the building, including a section known as the J.P. Bickell Gallery.[26] The festival filled a cultural void in Canadian society, providing a high-profile outlet for Canada's serious stage actors. With a permanent theatre, replete with the traditional Elizabethan stage, Stratford took a giant step toward its towering position within Canada's theatrical landscape.

In its first two years, the Foundation also provided approximately $200,000 to hospitals engaged in training medical students and doctors. Also during its first two years, the Foundation underwrote $109,755 toward significant research projects at the University of Toronto, Queen's University, and Toronto's Connaught Medical Research Laboratories. As a result, a variety of innovative studies were undertaken, as a *Toronto Star* article attested in 1953:

> Important medical projects at the University of Toronto assisted by the J.P. Bickell foundation are: research by Dr. W.T. Mustard to determine how an empty heart survives coronary occlusion; investigation by Dr. James Key on means by which a new blood supply might be brought to heart muscles suffering a blood shortage as a result of coronary artery disease; a study by Dr. Ian B. MacDonald of the trans-plantation of the kidneys and other organs with the aid of drugs such as ACTH; and an experimental study by Dr. C.S. Hanes of the mechanism of protein synthesis and cell growth.[27]

On top of this, the Foundation established several scholarships and bursaries that amounted to a two-year total of $50,620.[28]

With each year, the actual dollar figure of Bickell's gifts rose. The University of Toronto, for instance, saw a sharp increase in 1957, as the *Globe and Mail* reported:

> Three grants from the J.P. Bickell Foundation to the University of Toronto head a list of gifts announced last night. One for $12,306 will be used for two Sanborn four-channel recorder for medical research; $4,500 for a project on diseases of the optic nerve directed by Dr. Lois Lloyd; and $12,000 for research in the Connaught Medical Research Laboratories under Dr. P.J. Moloney's direction.[29]

The Foundation, however, touched smaller organizations, too. The Jewish Vocational Service, for example, was officially adopted by the Bickell-endorsed Toronto Community Fund. The JVS Rehabilitation Workshop was established to provide vocational services and on-the-job counselling for those individuals experiencing "work adjustment problems."[30] The Foundation also made possible a revamping of the Royal Ontario Museum's geological displays in 1957. The $100,000 bestowed on the museum allowed for restyled galleries that sought to encourage future Canadian metallurgists. In his address at the grand opening, Ontario's Minster of Mines Philip Kelly remarked: "The late J.P. Bickell (of McIntyre Porcupine Mines), who was a giant in the story of Canadian mining, has left his mark in a very tangible way."[31] It seemed that even in death, Bickell continued to generate a measurable impact on Ontarians and Canadian society at large.

J.P.'s gift is truly one that keeps on giving, and while one of the funding limitations was that the income was to be granted in Ontario, hundreds of thousands of Canadians have benefited

from Bickell's original gift. In its first sixty years of existence, the
J.P. Bickell Foundation has donated an astonishing sum to charity. Indeed, 80 percent of the charities to which the Foundation
regularly donates to did not even exist in 1951. By 2011 the
initial $13 million had grown to $111.8 million, more than
eight times its original value. As a perpetual charitable foundation with grants made from income only, Bickell's foundation has, as of 2011, granted $133.5 million, over ten times the
initial value of the capital funds set aside by Bickell. Since its
inception, the Foundation has provided the Hospital for Sick
Children with approximately $70 million; medical research at
universities, research institutes, and hospitals throughout Ontario
with approximately $14 million; and scholarships for mining
students totalling approximately $7 million. The Foundation has
also approved nearly six thousand requests from various charities
totalling over $45 million since 1951.[32]

The Dream-Maker

Over the years Bickell collected an impressive assortment of pictures, paintings, and art pieces, which he bequeathed to the Art
Gallery of Ontario (AGO). J.P.'s eye for art was keen. One painting he bought for $800 was later valued at $20,000.[33] In 1928
Bickell was elected a member of the Council of the Art Gallery
of Toronto. Ten years later he became a founder-member of the
gallery. When he died, his bequest to the AGO was not limited
to the paintings and sculptures in his personal collection, but also
included various domestic and household articles. The AGO was
given the opportunity to choose what it wanted for its own collection and for the gallery's Grange House. The gallery chose sixteen
paintings, four prints, three sculptures, and various tapestries and
objets d'art. Today, some 112 items are listed in the gallery's official
John Paris Bickell catalogue.[34]

The gallery was particularly pleased with three of the paintings left by Bickell. These are the eighteenth-century English painter Sir Joshua Reynolds's portrait of renowned English politician and man of letters Horace Walpole; the Anglo-Welsh artist Frank Brangwyn's *The Tugboat*; and American landscape painter George Inness's *Landscape, Approaching Storm*. Reynolds's portrait of Walpole, which the artist painted in 1756, once belonged to Casa Loma's builder Sir Henry Pellatt. Bickell purchased the Reynolds for $2,700 when Pellatt was forced to liquidate his assets in 1924.[35]

Canadian art was well represented in Bickell's collection by three bronze works by painter-sculptor Marc-Aurèle de Foy Suzor-Coté. The AGO was able to add to its accession list through the funds made possible by Bickell's bequest. To honour his memory, the gallery purchased works by Canadian artists including Isabel McLaughlin, Will Ogilvie, and L.A.C. Panton, and a seventeenth-century still-life by the Flemish painter Frans Snyder.

The furniture from Bickell's bequest was used in various galleries throughout the AGO and the Grange House. It was specially donated to the historic Grange House in the 1970s when that building was undergoing restoration. Bickell's furniture had previously been in the AGO's original members' lounge.[36]

While J.P.'s worldly possessions were happily preserved, the direct effect that the man produced on the lives of various influential individuals is a part of his legacy that is in need of some maintenance. For some, it was as simple as hearing the sage's financial advice. For others, it was about procuring J.P.'s guidance and direction on all sorts of business matters. For others still — the luckiest ones — Bickell footed bills, paid up debts, and faithfully bankrolled dreams. And there were many lucky ones who went on to greatness with help from J.P.

Jack Kent Cooke was among this last group. Cooke became the owner of the baseball Toronto Maple Leafs in 1951. During his tenure, Cooke returned the Maple Leafs team to its rightful stature as one of the marquee franchises in senior-level baseball. The Leafs led the International League in attendance from 1952 through 1956. In fact, the team drew over three million fans in Cooke's first ten years and won four pennants, including the 1960 incarnation, which won one hundred games.

Bickell's association with Jack Kent Cooke transcended the Maple Leafs connection. He also provided the necessary financial backing for Cooke to buy Toronto radio station CKCL in 1945. At first Bickell wasn't looking to invest in any new ventures when Cooke brought his idea to the mining magnate. Once in his office, Cooke kept talking: "I talked about everything, even the height of the building.... I figured as long as I could keep him from saying 'no' I had a chance."[37] Bickell informed Cooke the day after that he would invest in his radio initiative.

Cooke changed the call letters to CKEY, hired on-air personalities such as Lorne Greene and Mickey Lester, and so began his long and storied career in media ownership. Cooke became an extremely wealthy man, owning, among other commodities, Washington's football franchise, the Los Angeles Lakers of the National Basketball Association, and the National Hockey League's Los Angeles Kings (Cooke was really the first to bring hockey to California), several cable companies, and, for a time, both the Chrysler Building and the *Los Angeles Daily News*. And he owed one of his biggest breaks to Bickell. As his son John K. Cooke explained:

> [CKEY] was immediately popular and highly profitable. At the end of the first year Mr. Bickell and the other investors told my father that the station should be his because of his work and wanted only their investment repaid. A lovely story, and I believe my father.[38]

J.P. believed in and supported many winners in his time. Cooke was only one of a large number of successful investments that Bickell made in people with a dream.

It is difficult to quantify the number of people that Bickell helped personally. Future media mogul Roy Thomson was another. When Thomson's Timmins newspaper and radio station building burned to the ground, it was Bickell who found the necessary loan capital to finance a new building.[39] There was also Allen Graham, the son of Dr. Joseph Graham and Eleanor (née Boyd) Graham. When Dr. Graham died Allen was only eleven. It was J.P. Bickell — the boy's godfather — who stepped in to provide the necessary funds to send the lad to J.P.'s old alma mater, St. Andrew's College, in 1927. Allen eventually graduated from medical school only a few months before becoming Lieutenant Graham. As a member of Canada's medical corps during the Second World War, Graham was captured by the Germans and spent the bulk of the war treating sick and dying soldiers in the POW camps in North Africa. For his bravery in saving lives on the battlefield, Graham was awarded the Military Cross.[40]

Bickell also invested in several institutions during his lifetime. He paid, for example, for the renovation of Old St. Andrew's Presbyterian Church in Niagara-on-the-Lake, which had been built in 1790.[41] After hearing about the financial troubles an Anglican Church in Haileybury was having, Bickell arranged for its mortgage to be covered.[42] Yet the one institution with which the Bickell name is most often associated is an establishment in northern Ontario that is primarily dedicated to bringing fun to children.

Camp Bickell on Chapman Lake effectively began in the aftermath of a failed camping trip. Percy Boyce, principal of the Schumacher Public School in 1939, took a group of boys on what would become a miserably wet outing. With the rains, however, an idea flowered. On hearing about the failed trip, McIntyre Porcupine manager Dick Ennis suggested the idea of a more permanent camp to Bickell. J.P. personally authorized funding for such a camp in only three days.[43] Bickell also arranged for the relocation of two old machine shops from the McIntyre Porcupine mine to serve as camping accommodations. For the camp's grounds, 240 acres were leased from the Caron family on Chapman Lake, some thirty-seven miles from Timmins. In 1947 the Red Cross donated a small hospital to the camp.[44] In 1949 Bickell donated five thousand dollars to buy the leased property outright. Five sleeping cabins for the children and an ice house were built to complement those two machine shops that had been rescued from demolition. The first five cabins were named during his lifetime after his friends: Cabin #1 – Best (Dr. Charles Best), Cabin #2 – Baxter (Beverly Baxter, MP), Cabin #3 – Bennett (R.B. Bennett, prime minister), Cabin #4 – Banting (Dr. Fredrick Banting), Cabin #5 – Beaverbrook (Max Aitken, Lord Beaverbook).

Later still, an infirmary and two additional cabins for children were added. In 1950 Camp Bickell was officially incorporated. It was, and still is, a non-profit and non-denominational children's charity. Under the direction of Joe Campbell, whose commitment has been unwavering as the executive director for the past thirty years, a massive expansion and renovation project was undertaken in 2000, resulting in what today is the Camp Bickell/J.P. Bickell Outdoor Centre.[45] Since that first five-thousand-dollar donation, the J.P. Bickell Foundation has contributed more than $1 million toward the expansion, improvement, and upkeep of Camp Bickell and its Outdoor Centre.

The construction of Camp Bickell was not the first time Bickell invested in the community where he made much of his fortune. J.P. believed that the miners who toiled in his mine deserved an arena as grand as Maple Leaf Gardens.[46] The McIntyre Community Building, affectionately known as the Mac, was built in 1938. It was a facility well ahead of its time, housing six curling rinks, six bowling alleys, a basketball court, meeting rooms,

Camp Bickell near Timmins, Ontario, summer 2016.

and a coffee shop. The Mac also had a seating capacity of 1,783 for hockey games.

Bickell laid the cornerstone at the opening ceremony on August 27, 1938. During the event, Bickell addressed the audience that had assembled for the opening:

> My friends … the management of the mine has always been conscious of the benefits derived from healthful athletics and it was with this in mind that the building of the rink was undertaken. This rink when completed will be equal in equipment to the Maple Leaf Gardens in Toronto and I wish to congratulate Dan Keeley, chairman of the building committee, and his associates, S.A. Wookey, Angus D. Campbell and Dr. D. Robson, for their efforts in directing its construction.[47]

As if bringing the then world-class arena to the area wasn't enough, Bickell announced during the ceremony that he was giving the Schumacher Lions Club three thousand dollars to wipe out its existing swimming pool debt. As Bickell explained:

> It would never have been possible except for the enthusiasm of [the Lions Club] members and the contributions made by the community at large.... [With the three thousand dollars] the Lions will be able to discharge their liabilities and go on with other work without being hindered by any debts.[48]

With trowel in hand, Bickell laid the first brick of a multi-purpose facility that would be both directly and indirectly responsible for the career trajectory of an impressive number of famous Canadians.

> "At the conclusion of his address the president ... and with a few deft strokes laid the first brick at the southwest corner of the building and rising to his feet repeated the customary "I declare this stone to be well and truly laid." Returning to the role of stone mason again, Mr. Bickell laid a cement block to be used in the inner wall in which he deposited a puck used in the now famous marathon game between Boston and Maple Leafs in 1933." Richard Ennis goes on to say, "He has been congratulating us on the way we have emulated the Gardens with our new rink here."[49]

True to his word, the arena was a scale model of Maple Leaf Gardens, replete with red, green, and blue seats. As the *Toronto Star* reported on January 2, 1940:

The building leaves little to be desired. In addition to the purely athletic features, a lounge, beautifully furnished with nine views on the curling rinks, separate lounges for men and women as well as ample dressing rooms, makes the combination unique over any similar club in Canada. An excellent and commodious restaurant with the very latest of equipment will cater to the inner needs of the men between their bowling, curling, skating and gym activity.[50]

As president of the mine and now honorary president of the McIntyre Curling Club, J.P. Bickell threw out the first ceremonial rock on the new sheet on December 30, 1939. Even in that first year, the club boasted the largest known membership — composed of mostly McIntyre Mine employees — of any individual curling club in the world. Not surprisingly, Bickell also donated one of the first annual trophies given out at the club.[51] The club

The House that Dreams Built *by Michael Davidson — painting of the McIntyre Community Centre.*

has several times represented Northern Ontario at national competitions, including the Brier.

In a show of appreciation, the employees who were to benefit from Bickell's generosity presented him with a ceremonial gold-plated pickaxe measuring fifteen inches by nine inches, with an inscription that reads:

> Presented to President J.P. Bickell by the Employees
> of the McIntyre Mine, Dec 30th, 1939

The Maple Leafs played several exhibition games at the Mac to the delight of hundreds of people who never got a chance to see big league hockey in Toronto. The "Big M" — Frank Mahovlich — cut his teeth at the Mac with the Schumacher Lions before the Leafs signed him and brought him south to Toronto. So too did Father Les Costello, a hockey-playing priest whose commitment to the betterment of his parish, Timmins, was unmatched. Costello, a.k.a. "the Flying Father," perfected his own brand of skating at the Mac. The legendary Bill Barilko, a Timmins native, was also familiar with the Mac. Barilko famously died as a result of a plane crash only four months after scoring the Stanley Cup–winning goal for the Maple Leafs in 1951. His body wasn't discovered for eleven years. The Leafs did not win the cup again until after Barilko's body was found. Adding to the eeriness, Barilko and his friend Dr. Henry Hudson began their ill-fated journey the day after Bickell's funeral.[52]

There were more than just hockey stars to come out of J.P.'s Mac. Two-time world champion and Olympic gold medallist figure skater Barbara Ann Scott also trained extensively at the Mac in a unique "Private Mirrored Room (PMR)" with artificial ice located just down the hall from the larger ice hockey and figure skating surface in preparation for various competitions. And local girl turned Canadian country legend Shania Twain

McIntyre Arena opening ceremonies in 1938, with the Toronto Maple Leafs putting on an exhibition game for the McIntyre Mine families and community members. J.P. Bickell is among the dignitaries in the middle of the lineup, fifth from left.

first learned some of her big-stage swagger playing at the Mac in front of a home crowd.

Yet, the Mac provided not just a launch-pad for so many sons and daughters of Timmins, Schumacher, and Porcupine; it became, like the building it was modelled after, a cultural touchstone. As *Timmins Daily Press* journalist Karen Bachmann attested in 2008, "The Mac is a building that helps define who we are as residents in this city. Without it, we would be very much poorer."[53] It was yet another example of how Bickell's investment in people and institutions served the greater good.

This gift to the community has developed careers that have reached the highest level of hockey in Canada, to hear it from the Vice-Chair of Hockey Canada, Mr. Ed Pupich:

As a young boy growing up in Schumacher, my friends and I lived at the MAC. We knew all of the stories of J.P. Bickell and his building of our arena and his ties to Maple Leaf Gardens. From my parents' home, I could see the Mac from our front window and always thought how lucky we were to have such a building. When the Toronto Maple Leafs came to Schumacher for an exhibition game and visited the Public School – we were in awe and instant Leaf fans. As we grew older, and earned money at the Mac – setting pins in the bowling alley, cleaning the ice, sweeping the seats, putting in the floor over the ice pad for wrestling and roller skating and numerous other jobs we realized that activities at the MAC not only entertained us but were the means of receiving an allowance. We were RICH!!! In the summer, we all attended Camp Bickell, first as campers than as summer labourers. J.P. Bickell's vision was something that we in Schumacher were not only appreciative of, but that we were the envy of all of Northern Ontario. The MAC helped to put Schumacher on the map and has kept it there for over 70 years. As a Vice Chairman of Hockey Canada, I was fortunate enough to be able to bring to the MAC some International Hockey games and tournaments and able to "show off" the arena. People across Canada and from around the world are amazed that such a facility exists and that it is 70 years old. I am ALWAYS proud to sing the praises of the MAC. I now sit on the Board of Camp Bickell, 62 years after attending as a camper for the first time. We have made many improvements but J.P.'s vision remains — a children's camp. Thank you, Mr. Bickell.[54]

Bickell the Builder

For his role in building the Canadian institution known as the Toronto Maple Leafs, J.P. Bickell was inducted into the Hockey Hall of Fame in 1978 in the Builders category.[55] J.P. was likewise inducted into the Canadian Mining Hall of Fame in 2000.[56]

Highlighting Mr. Bickell's contribution to the mining sector and nominating him into the Mining Hall of Fame and were Mr. Graham Farquharson, chairman of Strathcona Minerals Services Limited, and Mrs. W.B. Dix, past president of the Women's Association of the Mining Industry of Canada and wife of Mr. Dix who worked at the McIntyre Mine from 1928 to 1968 and retired as the mine's vice-president and treasurer.

In the words of Mr. Farquharson,

> the other important beneficiary of the Bickell Foundation has been the mining industry because of the funding for scholarships in mining industry disciplines that Mr. Bickell has specified and which to

Hockey Hall of Fame postcard honouring J.P. Bickell — part of a series commissioned in 1983.

date [1999] has amounted to more than $3 Million.
As Chairman of the Canadian Mineral Industry
Education Foundation I can certainly attest to the
great importance of the annual contribution of
$20,000 we have received from the Bickell
Foundation for many years. Since the creation of the
Canadian Mineral Industry Education Foundation
in 1964 the J.P. Bickell Foundation has been, by far,
the largest single contributor.[57]

While there may not exist monuments erected to his name
"from the Yukon to the financial districts of Toronto and Montreal"
(as the *Globe and Mail* confidently predicted upon his passing),
J.P. Bickell's influence on Canadian society is not slight, and it
steadily endures.[58]

*Author Graham MacLachlan receiving, on behalf of the Bickell family,
an award honouring J.P. Bickell in the Builder Category, in the newly
opened Timmins Sports Heritage Hall of Fame, June 21, 2014.*

There is a laundry list of names that all, in varying degrees, owe a debt to Bickell. Nathanson and his Famous Players, Thomson and his newspaper empire, Smythe and the Maple Leafs, Cooke, Graham, Ennis, Rogers, and many others benefited from their friendship with J.P. Yet a greater number of not-so-famous and not-at-all famous Canadians owe Bickell his due as well. By 2004, just over fifty years since the organization was established, the J.P. Bickell Foundation had distributed over $100 million to charity. (Now, in 2017, the Foundation to date has contributed approximately $160,000 to various charities around Ontario.) This remarkable legacy has improved legions of Canadian lives. "Smiling Jack's" gift serves as inspiration not only to the modern multi-millionaire, but also to Canadians of any income who may be considering planned giving. Bickell would likely agree that even the most modest gift can effect positive change.[59]

Certainly, J.P.'s was an attractive personality. Courageous — at times strident — Bickell treasured adventure and chance.

Author Graham MacLachlan and his son Evan MacLachlan at the Hockey Hall of Fame, Toronto, November 2017. J.P. Bickell's plaque is at the far left, second row from the top.

Portrait of J.P. Bickell, by Joshua Smith, 1927.

He was also possessed of an independent mind and character. This spirit anchored Bickell, who, despite the political might and commercial weight that sometimes emanated from the influential friends circling within his orbit, was resolutely hard to sway. Perhaps the characteristic that best describes the reverend's son from Molesworth, however, is benevolence. When considering the sheer number of lives that J.P. Bickell touched during his lifetime and during the sixty-some years after his passing, any marks that may have blemished his character have since been thoroughly overshadowed by the copious portions of kindness and generosity that so distinguished this stout champion of the mining industry.

Acknowledgements

From Jason Wilson and Kevin Shea

Following the career trajectory of John Paris Bickell has proven to be a very satisfying journey. Tracing the steps of Bickell's broad footprints, not to mention his wide-ranging endeavours and diverse philanthropic commitments, presented a daunting task for the authors. Yet the journey remained satisfying and agreeable in no small measure due to the tremendous spade work already completed by Graham MacLachlan. Graham, Bickell's first cousin, was truly the driving force behind this book. He has carried the flame, shaken the trees, collected the necessary data, made the calls, and somehow found a way to make this book happen long before either of the authors got involved. By extension, Graham had already meticulously sourced the lion's share of materials, photographs, and personal items used in the research of this book. He certainly made our collective job a great deal more manageable. For all of these efforts and the inspiration, we are extremely grateful.

We are likewise grateful to David Windeyer. David is now a member of the Management Committee of the J.P. Bickell

Foundation, and he formerly managed the Foundation for both National Trust and later Scotia Trust. Thankfully for us, David was able to advance our mission through his intimate connections and personal experience with the J.P. Bickell Foundation. Additionally, we are grateful to Malcolm Burrows, initially for his work during his time at SickKids Hospital and in the creation of the J.P. Bickell Society, and now as Head, Philanthropic Advisory Services at Scotia Wealth Management.

We are also sincerely grateful and indebted to Scotiabank on behalf of the J.P. Bickell Foundation and to John W. Doig, Chief Marketing Officer of the Global Marketing division of Scotiabank and the Global Marketing team.

Thanks to Margaret Blenkhorn, archivist at the CIBC Archives, for her judicious efforts on our behalf. And to Kate McLaren and Christine Fortin from the Reference Department at the Timmins Public Library, who were extremely helpful in tracking down long-lost articles relating to J.P. We are likewise indebted to Lea Hill, the archivist and long-time member of the Mississaugua Golf and Country Club; Beverley Darville, staff archivist at the Royal Canadian Yacht Club; Amy Furness and Marilyn Nazar at the Art Gallery of Ontario; Jennifer Rieger, manager of the Grange House; Teruko Kishibe of St. Michael's Hospital; Ani Orchanian-Cheff of the University Health Network; Malcolm Berry, David Wencer, and Elizabeth Uleryk from the Hospital for Sick Children; Becky Bays from the Canadian Mining Hall of Fame; Karen Bachmann from the Timmins Museum; Sue Hayter from St. Andrew's College; Carolin Brooks from the Owen Sound and North Grey Union Public Library; Martin Wright, a true Maple Leafs historian and collector; Bobby Burrell from the Vintage Hockey Collector; and Fran Stewart from White Lake, Ontario.

While J.P. Bickell had no children or even nieces or nephews, we were delighted by the colour added by way of personal interviews that we conducted with Jim Smith, son of Bernard E.

Smith, Ed Pupich, Vice-Chair Hockey Canada, John Cooke (son of Jack Kent Cooke), and Anne Logan (daughter of Sydney H. Logan). Anne attested to Bickell's sense of horseplay; it appears that J.P. was caught feeding two-year-old Anne a far too liberal amount of bacon while she was still in her playpen. Her mother Hilda was not amused.

Every author knows well the importance of a solid support team at home, a team that is understanding and patient, especially in the wee hours of the morning when finding the right turn of phrase is a task rendered more manageable by a simple kiss to the head. We are lucky to have Alana and Nancy to give us said kisses (and to tell us to get to bed already!).

Finally, we'd like to thank J.P. Bickell for revealing himself to us. Certainly, his was a recognizable name long associated with our favourite team, the Toronto Maple Leafs. We had seen Bickell's name referenced several times in our impressive, if dusty, collection of old hockey books. Familiar as we were with the Leafs' grand narrative and the various Conn Smythe biographies, we knew that name had something to do with the embryonic stages of our blessed team. We were likewise aware of the J.P. Bickell Memorial Award, yet far less certain as to what — given its intermittent appearance over the last fifty years — it was actually awarded for. Fortunately, our crash course in *Bickellology* has gone some way in correcting our misapprehensions. We see now Bickell the man. We see the mining magnate who brought thousands of jobs to Canadians. We see the architect and facilitator of so many diverse and purposeful dreams. We see the relentless "Busy B" working on behalf of the Allies during the Second World War. And we see, and are humbled by, the supremely generous man who left his millions to help better the lives of others. It was, for us, a striking revelation that happily complicates our previous understanding of "that name." We hope you see it, too.

From Graham MacLachlan

The inspiration for this book has come from a number of sources each of which is important to acknowledge.

Obviously, the man at the centre of this book had an unimaginable career. To this day through his philanthropic endeavours he has touched so many who have provided great inspiration. Thank you, J.P. Bickell, for everything!

I would first like to thank the Dix family, initially William Bradley Dix, who was the president of the McIntyre Research Foundation (a non-profit medical foundation) and the vice-president and treasurer of the McIntyre Porcupine Mines Ltd. It was Mr. Dix whose life's work centred on the McIntyre Mine; he kept impeccable records and, in his own words, inspired the conscientious "string-saving habits" that governed the mine's operations. He loyally served as the executor for first J.P. Bickell (1951) and secondly Marjorie (Bickell) Paulin (1977), J.P.'s sister. For his efforts we are eternally grateful. Mr. Dix deserves a big thank-you on behalf of our family.

It was W.B. Dix's son Bradley Dix who then became the custodian of these records and preserved them for the next generation and Bickell family members, myself included. Mrs. Zandra Dix was kind enough to pass along all of these records and artifacts, preserving them forever in our family. These documents and pictures were essential to the telling of this story. So to you also, thank you.

I thank Balmer Neilly, Marsh Cooper, and his nephew David Etherington for caring for and preserving J.P. Bickell's sterling silver cigar box, a valued gift from the Toronto Maple Leafs board of directors.

I thank the people of Timmins/Schumacher/South Porcupine, Joe Campbell, and the board of directors of Camp Bickell for continuing to perpetuate J.P. Bickell's gift to the community.

I thank everyone at the Hospital for Sick Children in Toronto for their efforts in using J.P. Bickell's annual gift for the priceless work that they do and for every courtesy they have extended to me.

I would like to thank the people at Sportsnet, Scotiabank, and Rogers Hometown Hockey for making the journey to the McIntyre Arena and Recreation Complex in Timmins, Ontario, on November 26 and 27, 2016, to honour J.P. Bickell, Bill Barilko, and Frank Mahovlich. Making this possible were Wayne Bozzer, president of the Timmins Sports Heritage Hall of Fame, and Mayor Steve Black. The story narrated by Scott Morrison and on air with Ron MacLean and Tara Slone was right on point. Thank you.

Lastly, and most importantly, I would like to thank my immediate family Anika, Evan, and Rylan, and my extended family for your dedication, support, and inspiration to help me make this project a reality.

Sincerely,
Graham MacLachlan

Appendix

The J.P. Bickell Memorial Award

Since its inception, the J.P. Bickell Memorial Award was been presented to the following recipients:

1953	Ted Kennedy
1954	Harry Lumley
1955	Ted Kennedy
1956	Tod Sloan
1959	George Armstrong and Bob Pulford
1960	Johnny Bower
1961	Red Kelly
1962	Dave Keon
1963	Dave Keon
1964	Johnny Bower
1965	Johnny Bower
1966	Allan Stanley
1967	Terry Sawchuck
1969	Tim Horton
1971	Bobby Baun

1972	King Clancy
1979	Mike Palmateer
1993	Doug Gilmour
1995	Bob Davidson
1999	Mats Sundin and Curtis Joseph
2003	Pat Quinn

The award has been given out twenty-one times in its history of more than sixty years.

Notes

Introduction: A Life in Full

1. "Obituary: John Paris Bickell," *Globe and Mail* (24 August 1951), 6.
2. "Miners' Mart," *Time* 29.14 (5 April 1937), 93–98.
3. "Close Calls 6 Times, Bachelor Millionaire J.P. Bickell, 66, Dies," *Toronto Telegram* (23 August 1951), 3.
4. Anne M. Logan, *From Tent to Tower: The Biography of Sydney H. Logan* (Toronto: self-published, 1974), 110.
5. "Close Calls 6 Times," *Toronto Telegram*, 3.
6. "Leader in Mining and Finance J.P. Bickell Passes," *Northern Miner* (30 August 1951), 4.
7. J.P. Bickell Foundation, "A Four-Year Report to August 2011" (Toronto: J.P. Bickell Foundation, 2011), 27.

Chapter 1: Gold

1. For further discussion, see Alexander Grant, *Independence and Nationhood: Scotland 1306–1469* (Edinburgh: Edinburgh UP, 1984).

2. Kenneth Norrie and Douglas Owram, *A History of the Canadian Economy* (Toronto: Harcourt Brace Jovanovich Canada, 1991), 212–14.

3. Genealogical files courtesy of Graham MacLachlan.

4. Ibid., David Bickell death certificate.

5. "Announcements," *Huron Expositor* (13 February 1891), edition cover page.

6. "Financier, Mining Magnate, J.P. Bickell Stricken," *Globe and Mail* (23 August 1951), 10.

7. "Leader in Mining and Finance," *Northern Miner*, 4.

8. "A Backward Glance," *The Review* (Toronto: St. Andrew's College, 1901); Sue Hayter, "J.P. Bickell: Class of 1902," Andrean 56.2 (Fall 2012), 25; *The Review* (Toronto: St. Andrew's College, Christmas 1951), 87.

9. From Bickell's registration card at St. Andrew's College as quoted in Hayter, "J.P. Bickell: Class of 1902," 25.

10. Hayter, "J.P. Bickell: Class of 1902," 25.

11. "Financier, Mining Magnate," *Globe and Mail.*

12. "J.P. Bickell: 'Double or Nothing,'" *Star Weekly* [Toronto] (29 December 1951).

13. In 1906, Annie Bickell was living at 140 Robert Street. See *Toronto City Directory 1906.*

14. "Variety Spice of Existence for President of McIntyre," *Toronto Star* (8 November 1930).

15. "J.P. Bickell: 'Double or Nothing,'" *Star Weekly.*

16. *Toronto City Directory 1913.*

17. "J.P. Bickell: 'Double or Nothing,'" *Star Weekly.*

18. "F.J. Crawford CBC Governor By Order-in-Council," *Ottawa Journal* (22 November 1943).

19. George L. Cook with Marjorie Robinson, "'The Fight of My Life': Alfred Fitzpatrick and Frontier College's Extramural Degree for Working People," *Histoire sociale / Social History* 23.45 (May 1990), 81–112.

20. Alfred Fitzpatrick, *The University in Overalls: A Plea for*

Part-Time Study (Toronto: Thompson Educational Publishing, 1920), 22, 85.

21. Cook, "'The Fight of My Life,'" 85; "J.P. Bickell: 'Double or Nothing,'" *Star Weekly*.

22. See, for example, *Barthelmes v. Bickell*, 1921 62 S.C.R. 599 (Supreme Court of Canada, 9 December 1921). For another example of a case relating to foreign exchange rates, see *J.P. Bickell & Co. v. Cutten*, 1925 19 (Ontario Court of Appeals, 6 April 1925).

23. "Variety Spice of Existence," *Toronto Star*.

24. "J.P. Bickell Sells Out: Stock Broking Business Taken Over by A.L. Hudson & Co.," *Toronto Star* (16 March 1920), 23.

25. Philip Smith, *Harvest from the Rock: A History of Mining in Ontario* (Toronto: Macmillan of Canada, 1986), 128.

26. R. Douglas Francis, Richard Jones, and Donald B. Smith, *Destinies: Canadian History Since Confederation*, 6th ed. (Toronto: Nelson Education, 2008), 145–46.

27. Ibid., 145.

28. D.M. LeBourdais, *Metals and Men: The Story of Canadian Mining* (Toronto: McClelland & Stewart, 1957), 156–57.

29. Arnold Hoffman, *Free Gold: The Story of Canadian Mining* (New York and Toronto: Rinehart, 1947), 198.

30. Clary Dixon, as quoted in Hoffman, *Free Gold*, 199. See also, Karen Bachmann, "Dome Mine discovery made 100 years ago," *Daily Press* [Timmins, ON] (6 June 2009).

31. LeBourdais, *Metals and Men: The Story of Canadian Mining*, 163.

32. Smith, *Harvest from the Rock*, 187.

33. Hoffman, *Free Gold*, 199.

34. Clary Dixon, as quoted in Hoffman, *Free Gold*, 199.

35. Ibid.

36. LeBourdais, *Metals and Men: The Story of Canadian Mining*, 164.

37. Clary Dixon, as quoted in Hoffman, *Free Gold*, 199.

38. Ibid.

39. "J.P. Bickell: 'Double or Nothing,'" *Star Weekly*.

40. Smith, *Harvest from the Rock*, 192.

41. Ibid.

42. Bickell also became interested in the developments around the Cobalt mine, acquiring them from Sir Henry Pellatt for McIntyre Porcupine Mines Limited. See Smith, *Harvest from the Rock*, 193.

43. Ibid.

44. LeBourdais, *Metals and Men: The Story of Canadian Mining*, 163.

45. "Variety Spice of Existence," *Toronto Star*.

46. Hoffman, *Free Gold*, 199.

47. "Advertisement," *Evening Telegram* [New York] (17 April 1916), 11.

48. "Mr. J.P. Bickell Becomes New President of McIntyre," *Porcupine Advance* (7 February 1917), 7.

49. "J.P. Bickell: 'Double or Nothing,'" *Star Weekly*.

50. LeBourdais, *Metals and Men: The Story of Canadian Mining*, 263.

51. "J.P. Bickell: 'Double or Nothing,'" *Star Weekly*.

52. Ontario Department of Mines, *Annual Report* 45.1 (1936) (Toronto: T.E. Bowman, 1937), 132–35.

53. "John Paris Bickell," Inductee 2000, The Canadian Mining Hall of Fame, www.mininghalloffame.ca.

54. Smith, *Harvest from the Rock*, 193.

55. Forrest Davis, "Sell 'Em Ben Smith: The Epic of a Rover Boy in Wall Street," *Saturday Evening Post* 211.32 (4 February 1939), 14–15, 45–48, 50.

56. Ibid., 15, 45.

57. "Smith, Missing with Hepburn, Known in Wall Street as 'Sell 'Em Ben,'" *Citizen-Advertiser* [Auburn, NY] (28 July 1938), edition cover page.

58. Davis, "Sell 'Em Ben Smith," 14.

59. Ibid., 47.

60. During the war, Garfield Weston did his part for Beaverbrook and the Four B's. Moved by the sacrifice of so many Allied pilots, Weston handed Beaverbrook a blank cheque toward replacing lost aircraft. Beaverbrook, moved to tears, filled in an amount of £100,000 and assured Weston that his generous donation would raise many times more. "Britain's Biggest Baker: George Weston Limited" (company history), www.weston.ca.

61. Ibid.

62. "F.J. Crawford," *Ottawa Journal*.

63. Arthur St. L. Trigge, *A History of The Canadian Bank of Commerce*, with an account of the other banks which now form part of its organization, vol. 3: 1919–1930 (Toronto: The Canadian Bank of Commerce, 1934), 203.

64. The Pantages, which boasted a seating capacity of 3,500, cost approximately $600,000 to complete.

65. "Forms Canada Company," *New York Clipper* (5 March 1919), 32.

66. "Théâtre St-Denis' owners and tenants over the years," Théâtre St-Denis, official website, www.theatrestdenis.com.

67. "Variety Spice of Existence," *Toronto Star*.

68. Robert M. Seiler and Tamara P. Seiler, *Reel Time: Movie Exhibitors and Movie Audiences in Prairie Canada, 1896 to 1986* (Edmonton: Alberta U Press, 2013), 179; *Moving Picture World* (10 June 1916); *Globe* (24 August 1916), 2; *Toronto World* (25 August 1916), 7; *Toronto Daily News* (26 August 1916), 2; *Toronto Daily Star* (26 August 1916), 3; *Toronto Mail and Empire* (26 August 1916), 38; Peter White, *Investigation into an Alleged Combine in the Motion Picture Industry in Canada* (Ottawa: King's Printer, 1931), 16–20.

69. Seiler and Seiler, *Reel Time*, 180.

70. "Advertisement for the formal opening of the Regent Theatre," *Toronto Mail and Empire* (25 August 1916), 6; Seiler and Seiler, *Reel Time*, 180–81.

71. For further discussion on the ties between Famous Players and Paramount, see Paul S. Moore, "Nathan L. Nathanson Introduces Canadian Odeon: Producing National Competition in Film Exhibition," *Canadian Journal of Film Studies* 12.2 (Fall 2003), 22–45.

72. Seiler and Seiler, *Reel Time*, 184.

73. "Toronto Gets New House," *New York Clipper* (28 January 1920), 7.

74. Seiler and Seiler, *Reel Time*, 197.

75. Jason Wilson, *Soldiers of Song: The Dumbells and Other Canadian Concert Parties of the First World War* (Waterloo: Wilfrid Laurier UP, 2012).

76. "Allens of Canada in Difficulties; Creditors to Meet — Big Sums Involved," *The Film Daily* 20.54 (24 May 1922), edition cover page.

77. "J.P. Bickell: 'Double or Nothing,'" *Star Weekly*.

78. Heather Robertson, *Driving Force: The McLaughlin Family and the Age of the Car* (Toronto: McClelland & Stewart, 1995), 244–45.

Chapter Two: Risk

1. "Financier, Mining Magnate," *Globe and Mail*.

2. "J.P. Bickell: 'Double or Nothing,'" *Star Weekly*.

3. Ibid.

4. "Poker Debt: Case Recalls Big Games of Long Ago," *Globe and Mail* (26 October 1946), 17.

5. Ibid.

6. "Old Poker Debt Appeal Quashed," *Globe and Mail* (19 June 1947), 5.

7. "Variety Spice of Existence," *Toronto Star*.

8. Royal Canadian Yacht Club, *By-Laws: Regulations and List of Members of the Royal Canadian Yacht Club* (May 1911).

9. "Motor Boating," *Sporting Life* (11 September 1915), 34.

10. "Variety Spice of Existence," *Toronto Star*.

11. "The Syndicate," *Toronto Daily Star* (22 June 1920), 22.

12. "Miss Toronto II in Gold Cup Series," *Toronto Daily Star* (25 August 1920), 23.

13. Ibid.

14. Lou E. Marsh, "Buffalo Boat Upset, Sank in 70 Ft. Water," *Toronto Daily Star* (26 August 1920), 11.

15. "J.P. Bickell: 'Double or Nothing,'" *Star Weekly*.

16. "Financiers May Visit This City," *Evening Independent* [St. Petersburg, FL] (28 December 1927), 3.

17. "Financier, Mining Magnate," *Globe and Mail*.

18. Davis, "Sell 'Em Ben Smith," 15.

19. "Financier, Mining Magnate," *Globe and Mail*.

20. "Close Calls 6 Times," *Toronto Telegram*, 3.

21. "J.P. Bickell: 'Double or Nothing,'" *Star Weekly*.

22. Ibid.

23. "Close Calls 6 Times," *Toronto Telegram*, 3.

24. "On Aerial Trip to Hudson Bay: J.P. Bickell, McIntyre President, and Ben Smith Visiting in North," *Porcupine Advance* (29 August 1938), 1.

25. "Obituary: Bruce Victor Gibson — October 5, 2011," Air Canada Family, official website, www.acfamily.net.

26. Aerial Visuals: Airplane Dossier, official website, www.aerial-visuals.ca.

27. Watson Sellar, "Ottawa Goes to War," *Ottawa Journal* (24 September 1960), 31.

28. The plane swapped hands several times and is now, at the time of writing, owned by singer-songwriter Jimmy Buffett.

29. "Financier, Mining Magnate," *Globe and Mail*.

30. See "By-Law Number 57," *Official Records of the Mississauga*

Golf and Country Club Limited (Mississauga, ON: 19 April 1937), 163A, 163B.

31. John E. Hall, Evelyne Cassan, and Bettie Bradley, *Mississauga Golf and Country Club: 1906–1981, 75th Anniversary Book* (Mississauga, ON: Mississaugua Golf and Country Club, 1981), 41.

32. "J.P. Bickell: 'Double or Nothing,'" *Star Weekly*.

33. Ibid.

34. Hall, Cassan, and Bradley, *Mississaugua Golf and Country Club: 1906–1981*, 28.

35. "'Hole-in-One' Returns Santa Claus Fund $108: J.P. Bickell's Balloons Bring Happiness to Many Children," *Toronto Daily Star* (12 November 1925).

36. "Leader in Mining and Finance," *Northern Miner*, 4.

37. "J.P. Bickell Offers Belt for Feathers," *Toronto Daily Star* (10 September 1919).

38. Rose M. MacLeod, *The Story of White Cloud, Hay and Griffith Islands* (Richardson, Bond & Wright, 1979); Heather Robertson, *Driving Force*.

39. Gordon Macauley, *Daily Sun-Times* [Owen Sound] (1945).

Chapter 3: Ice

1. Frank J. Selke with Gordon Green, *Behind the Cheering* (Toronto: McClelland & Stewart, 1962), 80.

2. The O'Brien Cup, or O'Brien Trophy as it is sometimes referred to, was used by the NHA and later by the National Hockey League until 1950. It was awarded for a variety of designations: From 1910 until 1917, the cup was awarded to the NHA's champion; from 1921 until 1927 to the NHL playoff champion; from 1927 until 1938 to the NHL Canadian Division champion; and from 1939 until 1950 to the NHL playoff runner-up.

3. For further discussion on the Renfrew team, see Frank Cosentino, *The Renfrew Millionaires: The Valley Boys of Winter 1910* (Burnstown, ON: General Store Publishing House, 1990).

4. For more, see Morey Holzman and Joseph Nieforth, *Deceptions and Doublecross: How the NHL Conquered Hockey* (Toronto: Dundurn Press, 2002).

5. "Daily Star Trophy for K. & S. Team," *Toronto Daily Star* (4 April 1924).

6. Kelly McParland, *The Lives of Conn Smythe: From the Battlefield to Maple Leaf Gardens* (Toronto: Fenn / McClelland & Stewart, 2012), 82–83.

7. "St. Pats' Hockey Club in New Hands," *Toronto Daily Star* (9 December 1924), 10.

8. "Biography: J.P. Bickell," *Builders, Legends of Hockey*, official website of the Hockey Hall of Fame, www.legendsof hockey.net.

9. Selke with Green, *Behind the Cheering*, 76.

10. McParland, *The Lives of Conn Smythe*, 77.

11. Ibid.

12. W.A. Hewitt, "Sporting Views and Reviews," *Toronto Daily Star* (11 February 1927), 12.

13. Jim Vipond, "Week's Training Should Determine Successful Maple Leaf Candidates," *Globe and Mail* (30 September 1946), 20.

14. McParland, *The Lives of Conn Smythe*, 78–79.

15. See *Globe and Mail* (15 February 1927); *Toronto Star* (15 February 1927); McParland, *The Lives of Conn Smythe*, 78–79.

16. This encompasses Anglican, Baptist, Methodist, and Presbyterian. See Ian Hugh MacLean Miller, *Our Glory and Our Grief: Torontonians and the Great War* (Toronto: U of Toronto P, 2002), 8. See also James Lemon, *Toronto Since 1918* (Toronto: James Lorimer, 1985), Tables VII–IX: 196–97; and Russell Field, "Constructing the Preferred Spectator: Arena Design and Operation and the Consumption of

Hockey in 1930s Toronto," *International Journal of the History of Sport* 25.6 (May 2008), 665.

17. Miller, *Our Glory and Our Grief*, 104–05.

18. For further discussion, see Holzman and Nieforth, *Deceptions and Doublecross.*

19. The society made the maple leaf its official emblem. For further discussion on Viger see Robert Rumilly, *Histoire de la Société Saint-Jean-Baptiste de Montréal: des patriotes au Fleurdelisé, 1834–1948*, Collection connaissance des pays québécois, 13 (Montreal: L'Aurore, 1975).

20. *The Maple-leaf, Canadian Annual*, 3 vols. (Toronto: Henry Rowsell, 1846–48), Toronto Reference Library.

21. James Paton Clarke, "Lays of the Maple Leaf, or, Songs of Canada" (Toronto: A.S. Nordheimer, c. 1853). See also, Hannaford Street Silver Band, Howard Cable, "The Lays of the Maple Leaf," *Northern Delights* (Burlington, ON: Opening Day Recordings 1996).

22. Jay Myers, *The Fitzhenry and Whiteside Book of Canadian Facts and Dates*, revised and updated by Larry Hoffman and Fraser Sutherland (Richmond Hill: Fitzhenry and Whiteside, 1991), 121.

23. For many years afterward, a consignment of maple leaves was sent to the regiment wherever it was serving to commemorate Confederation on each first of July. The 100th Regiment was a Canadian force that was initially raised to serve in India during the Indian Rebellion of 1857. Though the regiment never reached India, it was used as a safeguard against the Fenian Brotherhood when that group was active in the 1860s, and later during the Boer War when it became the 1st Battalion of the Prince of Wales' Leinster Regiment, or Royal Canadians. See Paul Cowan, "Canadians in Defence of the Raj, 1858," *Dorchester Review* 3.2 (Autumn/Winter 2013), 8–11.

24. "The Maple Leaf," Canadian Heritage, official website of the Canadian government.

25. Alexander Muir, "The Maple Leaf Forever," A Canadian National Song, words and music by Alexander Muir (Toronto: self-published, 1867).

26. "The Maple Leaf," Canadian Heritage.

27. Gleaned from the sporting references and pages of the *Globe* (1850s–1900).

28. So ubiquitous was the name that the Canadian 4th Division's concert party was dubbed the "Maple Leafs." See Wilson, *Soldiers of Song*, 54, 56.

29. Conn Smythe, speech given at the Toronto Maple Leaf club banquet (October 1945). Conn Smythe Fonds, Archives of Ontario; McParland, *The Lives of Conn Smythe*, 80.

30. Ibid.

31. Indeed, the Philadelphia Quakers, a franchise that had taken over the homeless Pittsburgh Pirates, lasted only one miserable season in Philadelphia. The Quakers' lone season was a disaster. The team won only four games during the forty-four-game NHL season of 1930–31. See Dan Diamond et al., "Franchise Histories: Philadelphia Quakers," *Total Hockey: The Official Encyclopaedia of the National Hockey League*, 2nd ed. (New York: Total Sports Publishing, 2000), 260–61.

32. For further discussion on the idea of "civilizing" the hockey watching experience at this time, see Russell Field, "'There's more people here tonight than at a first night of the Metropolitan': Professional Hockey Spectatorship in the 1920s and 1930s in New York and Toronto," Andrew Holman, ed., *Canada's Game: Hockey and Identity* (Montreal and Kingston: McGill-Queen's UP, 2009), 127–50.

33. McParland, *The Lives of Conn Smythe*, 83.

34. Russell Field, for instance, argued that Smythe, Bickell et al. hoped to "cloak" the predominantly male pastime of ice hockey in feminine norms of respectability to compete in the burgeoning entertainment economy of the late 1920s. See Field, "Constructing the Preferred Spectator," 649.

35. Selke with Green, *Behind the Cheering*, 92.

36. *Globe and Mail* (3 September 1930); McParland, *The Lives of Conn Smythe*, 84.

37. McParland, *The Lives of Conn Smythe*, 84.

38. Conn Smythe as quoted in David Mills, "The Blue Line and the Bottom Line: Entrepreneurs and the Business of Hockey in Canada, 1927–1990," Paul Staudohar and James A. Mangan, eds., *The Business of Professional Sports* (Urbana: U of Illinois P, 1991); William Houston, *Inside Maple Leaf Gardens: The Rise and Fall of the Toronto Maple Leafs* (Toronto: McGraw Hill-Ryerson, 1989), 14; Richard Gruneau and David Whitson, *Hockey Night in Canada: Sport, Identities and Cultural Politics* (Toronto: Garamond Press, 1993), 102.

39. J.P. Bickell, "President's Address to Sports Followers of the Queen City," *Maple Leaf Gardens Official Programme, Toronto Maple Leafs v. Chicago Black Hawks* (Toronto: 12 November 1931), 28.

40. "Nutsy Fagan" [Ted Reeve], *Official Hockey Program, Arena Gardens*, Fonds 70, Series 306, Subseries 1, File 23, City of Toronto Archives (November 1930); McParland, *The Lives of Conn Smythe*, 114.

41. Selke with Green, *Behind the Cheering*, 86.

42. Ibid., 87.

43. Field, "Constructing the Preferred Spectator," 657.

44. Ibid.

45. Geo. A. Ross, "Letter to Harry McGee," (21 May 1931), General Files of James Elliott, File M-103: "Maple Leaf Gardens: General Matters," F229–282, T. Eaton Co. Fond, Archives of Ontario; Field, "Constructing the Preferred Spectator," 660.

46. McParland, *The Lives of Conn Smythe*, 119.

47. Ibid.

48. Maple Leaf Gardens Limited, "Manuscript," placed in

the cornerstone of the Maple Leaf Gardens (Toronto: 21 September 1931).

49. Ibid.

50. Jamie Bradburn, "Historicist: Opening the Gardens," *The Torontoist* (14 November 2009).

51. Conn Smythe, as quoted in Milt Dunnell, "Speaking on Sport," *Toronto Daily Star* (29 August 1951), 14.

52. Ibid.

53. J.P. Bickell, as quoted in the *Mail and Empire* (21 September 1931); Bradburn, "Historicist," *Torontoist*.

54. Tony Bennett, *The Birth of the Museum: History, Theory, Politics* (London: Routledge, 1995), 47; Field, "Constructing the Preferred Spectator," 653.

55. "Diagrams Showing Types of Seats," 6 July 1931, Maple Leaf Gardens, 13-164-03M, Ross and Macdonald Archive, Canadian Centre for Architecture, Montreal; Drawing No. 3.01 B: First Floor Plan, Maple Leaf Gardens (2), RG 56-10 D-3330, Theatre Plans Archives of Ontario; Field, "Constructing the Preferred Spectator," 662–63.

56. "Washrooms at Maple Leaf Gardens," Maple Leaf Gardens (2), RG 56-10 D-330, Theatre Plans; Box K-663, F 223-2-1, Conn Smythe Fonds, Archives of Ontario.

57. In 1930s Toronto, over 80 percent of the people were of British ancestry. Moreover, two-thirds of non-native Torontonians were born in the United Kingdom. See Lemon, *Toronto Since 1918*, 196–97; Field, "Constructing the Preferred Spectator," 665.

58. Selke with Green, *Behind the Cheering*, 92.

59. "Ceremony and Action at Opening Night at Maple Leaf Gardens," *Globe* (13 November 1931), 11.

60. Edwin Allan, "Sporting Gossip," *Toronto Mail and Empire* (14 November 1931).

61. J.P. Fitzgerald, "Maple Leaf Gardens Formally Opened," *Toronto Telegram* (13 November 1931).

62. Selke with Green, *Behind the Cheering*, 93.

63. Foster Hewitt, as quoted in *The Longines Symphonette Society, Hockey Night in Canada* (Toronto: HNIC 1, c. 1971) (audio/ LP).

64. J.P. Bickell, "The President's Message to Maple Leaf Fans," *Maple Leaf Gardens Official Programme, Toronto Maple Leafs v. Montreal Maroons* (Toronto: 23 January 1934), 2; Field, "Constructing the Preferred Spectator," 663–64.

65. Bobby Hewitson, "Inside the Blue Line," *Toronto Telegra*m, 24 March 1937; Field, "Constructing the Preferred Spectator," 670.

66. Conn Smythe as quoted in Conn Smythe with Scott Young, *If You Can't Beat 'em in the Alley* (Toronto: McClelland & Stewart, 1981), 179. See also, McParland, *The Lives of Conn Smyth*e, 247–49.

67. The award was presented at the discretion of the Toronto Maple Leafs directors to a member of the Toronto Maple Leafs organization — including non-players — who demonstrated a high standard of excellence during a single season or over the course of a career.

68. "$10,000 J.P. Bickell Memorial Cup," *Globe and Mail* (29 August 1952), 15.

69. Ibid.; Gord Walker, "Gardens Signs 3-Year Pact Covering Both Radio and TV," *Globe and Mail* (19 June 1953), 21.

70. "Bickell Trophy to Be Presented to Kennedy Before Hawks' Tilt," *Toronto Daily Star* (10 October 1953).

71. "$10,000 Cup to Commemorate J.P. Bickell," *Toronto Maple Leaf Program*, Baxter Publishing (11 October 1952).

72. "Big Leaf Prize stays on shelf till Cup win," *Toronto Daily Star* (25 October 1977).

73. "Maple Leaf Gardens, History of Arena Built for Toronto Maple Leafs Hockey Team," Parliament of Canada, Debates of the Senate (Hansard) (4 March 1999).

Chapter 4: Extravagance

1. Trigge, *A History of The Canadian Bank of Commerce*, 203.
2. "Canadian Bank Directors," *New York Evening Post* (28 April 1928), F3.
3. "Thomson and McKinnon Brokers" [Advertisement], *Miami News* (15 December 1926), 18.
4. "J.P. Bickell: 'Double or Nothing,'" *Star Weekly*.
5. "Brokerage Firm to Open Office," *Sarasota Herald-Tribune* (27 February 1937), 9.
6. "J.P. Bickell: 'Double or Nothing,'" *Star Weekly*.
7. Ibid.
8. "Leader in Mining and Finance," *Northern Miner*, 4.
9. "Million Made by Howell in 'Corner' on July Corn," *Sandusky Register* (1 August 1931), 7.
10. "J.P. Bickell: 'Double or Nothing,'" *Star Weekly*.
11. "Canadian Banker Dies at Home in Toronto," *Fort Pierce News Tribune* (11 January 1953), 2.
12. Logan, *From Tent to Tower*, 109.
13. Ibid., 110.
14. Interview with Anne M. Logan (26 June 2014).
15. Francis, Jones, and Smith, *Destinies*, 299.
16. John T. Saywell, *"Just call me Mitch": The Life of Mitchell F. Hepburn* (Toronto: U of Toronto P, 1991), 4.
17. Canadian economist Harry Johnson, for example, confessed that there was "pressure from millionaires" in the Hepburn camp. See Harry Johnson as quoted in Saywell, "Just call me Mitch," 391.
18. A "wet" was in favour of repealing prohibition in Ontario, and stood opposed to the "dry" who wished to keep the act in place.
19. Saywell, "Just call me Mitch," 152–53.
20. Francis, Jones, and Smith, *Destinies*, 145.
21. Margaret Conrad and Alvin Finkel, *History of the Canadian*

Peoples: 1867 to the Present, vol. 2, 4th ed. (Toronto: Pearson Longman, 2006), 246.

22. McCullagh was acting on behalf of another mining magnate, William Henry Wright. McCullagh committed suicide in 1952.

23. Saywell, "Just call me Mitch," 251.

24. Ibid., 277.

25. Saywell, "Just call me Mitch," 407, 601.

26. Sir Anthony Jenkinson, *Where Seldom a Gun Is Heard* (London: Arthur Baker, 1937), 215; as reprinted in, Saturday Night (December 1937); Saywell, "Just call me Mitch," 408.

27. Saywell, "Just call me Mitch," 408.

28. Ibid.

29. Ibid., 409.

30. Interview with Anne M. Logan (26 June 2014).

31. Ibid.

32. Ibid.

33. Ibid.

34. Logan, *From Tent to Tower*, 110.

35. Interview with Anne M. Logan (26 June 2014).

36. "Leader in Mining and Finance," *Northern Miner*, 4.

37. Stan Davies, "You can have tycoon's mansion for $490,000," *Toronto Star* (15 July 1972); Paul A. Mitcham, "Proposed Heritage Designation Bickell Estate, 1993, 2009, and 2025 Mississauga road (Ward 8)," *Corporate Report* (Mississauga: 20 July 2007), Appendix 1: Designation Report, 2.

38. Mitcham, "Proposed Heritage Designation Bickell Estate," 2.

39. Sinaiticus, "An Appreciation," *Construction: A Journal for the Architectural Engineering and Contracting Interest of Canada* 20.5 (Toronto: May 1927), 156.

40. Paula Wubbenhorst, "Bickell Estate finally designated under the Ontario Heritage Act," *Heritage Planning* (c. 2007), www.mississauga.ca.

41. Mitcham, "Proposed Heritage Designation Bickell Estate," 4.

42. Gleaned in part from "Millionaire-Sportsman Completing $250,000 Residence at Port Credit," *Toronto Daily Star* (6 February 1931), 33.

43. "Library of J.P. Bickell Residence, Port Credit," *Construction: A Journal for the Architectural Engineering and Contracting Interest of Canada* 20.5 (Toronto: May 1927), 155.

44. The library won an honourable mention from the Royal Architectural Institute of Canada for "domestic interiors" at the Institute's Toronto Chapter Architectural Exhibition in 1929. See E.R. Arthur, "The Toronto Chapter Architectural Exhibition," *Journal of the Royal Architectural Institute of Canada* 6 (March 1929); Mitcham, "Proposed Heritage Designation Bickell Estate," 5.

45. Interview with Anne M. Logan (26 June 2014).

46. "Millionaire-Sportsman," *Toronto Daily Star*, 33.

47. "Variety Spice of Existence," *Toronto Star*.

48. "Bickell Home Said Sold for $175,000 to 'Group,'" *Toronto Star* (21 January 1952), 1–2; Mitcham, "Proposed Heritage Designation Bickell Estate," 3; "Bickell Mansion Sold for $150,444 to Mine Financier," *Globe and Mail* (22 January 1952), 5.

49. John Stewart, "Home from the Roaring '20s for sale at $4.9 million," *Mississauga News* (10 April 2005).

50. Saywell, "Just call me Mitch," 277.

51. Ibid., 302.

52. "Hepburn Visits Northern Mining Town," *Ottawa Journal* (19 May 1936).

53. Tim Buck, leader of Canada's Communist Party, and six other members were imprisoned in 1931. See Conrad and Finkel, *History of the Canadian Peoples*, 238.

54. Ibid.

55. Ibid.

56. However one evaluates his distaste for organizations such as the Congress of Industrial Organizations (CIO) and later

the United Auto Workers, Mitchell lost two cabinet ministers over the 1937 Oshawa strike in Arthur Roebuck and David Croll, who resigned in disgust. The premier had sent in "Hepburn's Hussars" — a government-supported police force — to break the strike, which prompted Croll to state that Hepburn's place should have been "marching with the workers rather than riding with General Motors." See Francis et al., *Destinies*, 299.

57. *New York Times, Globe and Mail, Toronto Daily Star* (19, 20 April 1937); Saywell, "Just call me Mitch," 327.

58. Globe and Mail (20 April 1937); Saywell, "Just call me Mitch," 327, 586.

59. Norman McLeod as quoted in Saywell, "Just call me Mitch," 327, 586.

60. *Toronto Daily Star* (16 July 1938); Saywell, "Just call me Mitch," 388–89.

61. *Toronto Daily Star* (16 July 1938); Saywell, "Just call me Mitch," 389.

62. Saywell, "Just call me Mitch," 408–9.

63. "Flying Premier: Denies Arctic Trip Is Political Mission," *Winnipeg Free Press* (18 July 1938).

64. "Smith, Missing with Hepburn," *Citizen-Advertiser* [Auburn, NY], edition cover page.

65. Saywell, "Just call me Mitch," 389.

66. Ibid., 422.

67. Ibid., 452.

68. "Bickell Returns Home Optimistic on Outlook but Silent about Plans," *Globe and Mail* (15 August 1941), 4.

69. "Colin Campbell to Mitchell Hepburn," Hepburn Papers (15 September 1940); Saywell, "Just call me Mitch," 453, 609.

70. Ibid.

71. Ibid., 534.

Chapter Five: War

1. "Firm Make Known Year-End Changes: John P. Bickell Leaves Thomson & McKinnon as Senior Partner Today," *New York Times* (31 December 1938).
2. Davis, "Sell 'Em Ben Smith," 15.
3. "J.P. Bickell: 'Double or Nothing,'" *Star Weekly*.
4. For further discussion of Bickell and Beaverbrook's relationship, see The Beaverbrook Papers: Canadian Correspondence and Papers, Parliamentary Archives [London]; Lord Beaverbrook Fonds (London: Beaverbrook Library).
5. "J.P. Bickell Goes to London," *Ottawa Journal* (16 July 1940), edition cover page.
6. "Won Survival, Will Win Out, Says Bickell," *Globe and Mail* (15 October 1941), 4.
7. "Financier, Mining Magnate," *Globe and Mail*.
8. "'The Busy B'—Britain's Go-Getter," *Winnipeg Tribune* (29 January 1941), 7.
9. Several official exchanges between Beaverbrook and Bickell from late 1940 through the summer of 1941 survive in the Lord Beaverbrook Fonds (London: Beaverbrook Library).
10. "Won Survival," *Globe and Mail*, 4.
11. "Financier, Mining Magnate," *Globe and Mail*.
12. "Germans' Defeat in Air Certain Bishop Declares on Return," *Ottawa Journal* (7 October 1940), edition cover page, 19.
13. "J.P. Bickell Thinks Red Tape Something to Be Thrown Away," *Porcupine Advance* (26 June 1941), 3.
14. "J.P. Bickell's Brook Trout Pleases Palates in Britain," *Globe and Mail* (3 July 1941), 3.
15. Douglas Amaron, "Canada's Busy B's in Britain," *Globe and Mail* (19 March 1941), edition cover page.
16. Ibid.
17. "J.P. Bickell Dies; Mining Financier," *New York Times*

(23 August 1951). From the end of the war until the end of his days, Bickell cherished a portrait of Churchill that had a prominent place in his Mississauga mansion.

18. See William Fong, *J.W. McConnell: Financier, Philanthropist, Patriot* (Montreal and Kingston: McGill-Queen's UP, 2008).

19. I.A. McPhail, F.C. Biggar, and R.K. McCarthy, eds., "Ourselves," *The Caduceus, Staff Magazine of the Canadian Bank of Commerce* 22.1 (Toronto: The Canadian Bank of Commerce, January 1941), 1, 4.

20. H.R. Armstrong, "Bickell Doing 'Impossible Job' in Air Output," *Toronto Star* (26 July 1941).

21. Ibid.

22. Ibid.

23. "'Busy B' Bickell Controls U.K. Plane Ferry Service," *Winnipeg Tribune* (2 July 1941), 7.

24. "Bickell Returns Home," *Globe and Mail*, 4.

25. Ibid.

26. "Won Survival," *Globe and Mail*, 4.

27. "Taking Over New Task for Britain Says J.P. Bickell," *Ottawa Citizen* (15 August 1941), 15.

28. "Bickell Donates $5,000 to Air Force Benevolent Fund," *Ottawa Journal* (30 December 1942), 3.

29. Ibid.

30. "J.P. Bickell: 'Double or Nothing,'" *Star Weekly*; Logan, *From Tent to Tower*, 109.

31. "Victory Aircraft Head," *Financial Post* (31 July 1943).

32. John W. R. Taylor, *Combat Aircraft of the World: From 1909 to the Present* (New York: G.P. Putnam's Sons, 1969), 314.

33. For further discussion, see Martin Middlebrook, *The Battle of Hamburg: The Firestorm Raid* (London: Cassell Military Paperbacks, 2000).

34. *The Dam Busters*, directed by Michael Anderson (UK: Association British Pathé, 1955).

35. Adolf Galland, *The First and the Last: Germany's Fighter Force*

in WWII, Fortunes of War Series (Black Hawk, CO: Cerberus Press, 2005), 119.

36. Tony Iveson and Brad Milton, *Lancaster: The Biography* (London: Andre Deutsch, 2009), 82.

37. "Letter: J.P. Bickell to C.D. Howe," (21 October 1943); "Correspondence Tabled in Resignation of Victory Aircraft Head," *Globe and Mail* (12 February 1944), 7.

38. "Letter: C.D. Howe to J.P. Bickell," (30 October 1943); "Correspondence Tabled in Resignation," *Globe and Mail*, 7.

39. "Letter: J.P. Bickell to C.D. Howe," (26 November 1943); "Correspondence Tabled in Resignation," *Globe and Mail*, 7.

40. "Why Bickell Quit His Job," *Lethbridge Herald* (12 February 1944).

41. "Letter: C.D. Howe to J.J. Vaughan," (25 January 1944); "Correspondence Tabled in Resignation," *Globe and Mail*, 7.

42. "Leader in Mining and Finance," *Northern Miner*, 4.

43. Wellington Jeffers, "Finance at Large," *Globe and Mail* (21 May 1943), 22.

44. Ibid.

45. "U.S. Counsel Charges Laws Hurt Mining," *Globe and Mail* (2 October 1951), edition cover page.

46. Thomas A. Sutton as quoted in ibid.

47. "Minister Tours Turbojet Plant," *Globe and Mail* (16 September 1946), 2. Dobson would take over Bickell's position as chairman after Bickell died. See James Hornick, "Arms Production Chief Takes Over Job at Avro," *Globe and Mail* (12 October 1951), edition cover page.

48. James Dow, *The Arrow: The Dramatic Story of a Pioneering Canadian Aircraft Maker and Its Legendary Supersonic Fighter* (Toronto: James Lorimer, 1997), 25.

49. Ibid., 144.

50. "Avro Canadian Factory," *Flight* (29 November 1945), 573.

51. Mike Filey, "Canada Zoomed Ahead with Ambitious Jetliner,"

Toronto Sketches: "The Way We Were" (Toronto and Oxford: Dundurn Press, 1992), 158–59; originally printed as Mike Filey, "Canada Zoomed Ahead with Ambitious Jetliner," *Toronto Sun* (6 August 1989).

52. In 1954, the company became two separate subsidiaries. Avro Aircraft Limited, for instance, built the famous Avro Arrow and boasted over 25,000 employees. See Hayter, "J.P. Bickell: Class of 1902," 25. For further discussion on the Avro Arrow, see Dow, *The Arrow*.

53. "Don't Quote Me," *Toronto Star* (15 June 1945).

54. Excerpt from the Business Section, *Toronto Star* (30 May 1945). McIntyre Porcupine's subsidiary in Belleterre reported a net profit of $413,630 that same year.

55. J.P. Bickell, as quoted by Reid Taylor, "Only a Free Market for Gold Will Save the Nation," Congressional Record — Senate 14533 (Washington, DC: 16 August 1954).

56. William Henry Moore, *Yellow Metal* (Toronto: Printers Guild Limited, 1934).

57. "J.P. Bickell and His Faith in Gold," *Ottawa Journal* (23 June 1944), 8.

58. "Leader in Mining and Finance," *Northern Miner*, 4.

59. David Berman, "The trouble with gold: beaten up, but still no bargain," *Globe and Mail* (25 June 2014), B14.

60. Watt Hugh McCollum, *Who Owns Canada? An Examination of the Facts Concerning the Concentration of Ownership and Control of the Means of Production, Distribution and Exchange in Canada* (Ottawa: Woodsworth House Publishers, 1947), 9–10.

61. "Financier, Mining Magnate," *Globe and Mail*.

62. "Officers Elected by Metal Mines," *Globe and Mail* (28 May 1948), 22.

63. "National Mining Association Had Good First Year," *Globe and Mail* (4 June 1948), 24.

64. Logan, *From Tent to Tower*, 110.

65. "Leader in Mining and Finance," *Northern Miner*, 4.
66. "J.P. Bickell: 'Double or Nothing,'" *Star Weekly*.

Chapter 6: Benevolence

1. "John P. Bickell, 67, Dies, Funeral Service Saturday," *Toronto Daily Star* (23 August 1951), 14.
2. The Canadian Bank of Commerce, "Director's Report," *Annual Report* (Toronto: The Canadian Bank of Commerce, 1951).
3. National Trust Company Limited, "Minutes" (Toronto: National Trust Company Limited, 5 September 1951), 3.
4. "J.P. Bickell: 'Double or Nothing,'" *Star Weekly*.
5. Ibid.
6. Different numbers have been given for what Bickell's estate was actually worth, but these are not significantly different; they include $14,577,508.84 and $14,577,518. See "J.P. Bickell: 'Double or Nothing,'" *Star Weekly*; "Gives $14,577,518 to Charity," *Toronto Daily Star* (5 November 1951), edition cover page.
7. "J.P. Bickell Will Makes Hospital Main Beneficiary," *Globe and Mail* (6 November 1951), 5.
8. Tom O'Connor, *The Ladies' 1924-1999: A History of the Ladies' Golf Club of Toronto* (Toronto: Dundurn Press, 1999).
9. Personal family files courtesy of Graham MacLachlan.
10. J.P. Bickell, Last Will and Testament (Toronto: 2 February 1951), 1–6. From the personal family files of J.P. Bickell, courtesy of Graham MacLachlan.
11. Ibid.
12. The will included a special clause whereby the 50 percent slated for the Hospital for Sick Children would be added to the 35 percent to be distributed at the discretion of the trustees should the hospital cease to exist. See "J.P. Bickell Will," *Globe and Mail*, 5.

13. "Bickell Will Gives Huge Sum to Charity," *Ottawa Journal* (12 November 1951), 6.

14. "J.P. Bickell: 'Double or Nothing,'" *Star Weekly*.

15. G.C. Brink, "How Pasteurization of Milk Came to Ontario," *Canadian Medical Association Journal* 91 (31 October 1964), 972–73.

16. Ibid., 973.

17. "Savants Test Aluminum as Silicosis Preventive," *Utica Observer Dispatch* (5 November 1937), 8.

18. "J.P. Bickell: 'Double or Nothing,'" *Star Weekly*.

19. The McIntyre Research Foundation ceased operations in 1992. For further discussion, see The McIntyre Research Foundation Fonds (1930–1992), Archives of Ontario.

20. Logan, *From Tent to Tower*, 110.

21. "Variety Spice of Existence," *Toronto Star*.

22. "Generous Gift to Schumacher Red Cross," *Porcupine Advance* (2 October 1918), 1.

23. "J.P. Bickell: 'Double or Nothing,'" *Star Weekly*.

24. "More Ways to Give," SickKids Foundation, official website of SickKids Foundation. www.sickkidsfoundation.com.

25. J.P. Bickell Foundation, "A Four-Year Report," 10.

26. "Stratford Theatre Receives Gift of $100,000," *Globe and Mail* (24 January 1956), edition cover page, 17.

27. "J.P. Bickell Foundation Donations Hit $1,013,500," *Toronto Daily Star* (19 November 1953), 10.

28. "Foundation Gives 63 Organizations Financial Aid," *Globe and Mail* (19 November 1953), 4; "23 Organizations Receive Grants from Bickell Will," *Globe and Mail* (28 March 1952), 5; "Bickell Foundation Gives $480,000 in First Year," *Globe and Mail* (23 August 1952), 28.

29. "List of Gifts to University Is Announced," *Globe and Mail* (2 August 1957), 5.

30. "Individuals Assisted by Vocational Service," *Globe and Mail* (16 July 1957), 4.

31. "Museum Displays Seen Mine Study Incentive," *Globe and Mail* (16 February 1957), 9.

32. J.P. Bickell Foundation, "A Four-Year Report," 10, 12, 14–15.

33. "J.P. Bickell: 'Double or Nothing,'" *Star Weekly*.

34. The Art Gallery of Ontario, "Catalogue: John Paris Bickell" (Toronto: Art Gallery of Ontario, as of February 2012).

35. Peter Coffman, "Casa Loma and the Gothic Imagination," *Journal of the Society for the Study of Architecture in Canada* 3.4 (2003), 8.

36. Correspondence with Jennifer Rieger, manager of the Grange House (Toronto: 17 January 2013).

37. Jack Kent Cooke as quoted in Adrian Kinnane, *Jack Kent Cooke: A Career Biography* (Lansdowne, VA: Jack Kent Cooke Foundation, 2004), 16.

38. Interview with John K. Cooke (8 February 2014).

39. Michael Barnes, "Roy Thomson's Timmins Adventures," *Republic of Mining* (16 June 2008), www.republicofmining.com.

40. Sandra Martin, "Doctor won Military Cross for bravery in a raging tank battle in North Africa," *Globe and Mail* (7 December 2011).

41. "J.P. Bickell: 'Double or Nothing,'" *Star Weekly*.

42. Ibid.

43. "The Early Days of Camp Bickell," *Spirit of Schumacher*, 1 (February 2012), 5.

44. "Red Cross Donate Hospital to Camp," *Porcupine Advance* (24 July 1947), 5.

45. For more information, see Camp Bickell, official website, www.campbickell.com.

46. Kevin Shea, *Barilko: Without a Trace* (Toronto: Fenn, 2004), 5.

47. "Magnificent Building to Be Ready This Fall," *Porcupine Advance* (29 August 1938), 1, 7.

48. Ibid., 1.

49. See "Magnificent Building," *Porcupine Advance*, 7.

50. "McIntyre Building addition is dedicated by J.P. Bickell," *Toronto Star* (2 January 1940).

51. See "History of the McIntyre Curling Club," www.mcyintyre-curling.tripod.com/history.

52. For further discussion, see Shea, *Barilko*.

53. Karen Bachmann, "Jewel of the North still shines bright," *The Daily Press* (18 October 2008).

54. Ed Pupich, Letter to The J.P. Bickell Foundation, 29 September 2015.

55. "Biography: J.P. Bickell," *Legends of Hockey*.

56. "John Paris Bickell," The Canadian Mining Hall of Fame.

57. Ibid.

58. "Obituary: John Paris Bickell," *Globe and Mail*, 6.

59. "Plans evolve, and good banking advice is critical," *Globe and Mail* (12 July 2004), L7.

Bibliography

Primary Sources

Books

Fitzpatrick, Alfred. *The University in Overalls: A Plea for Part-Time Study*. Toronto: Thompson Educational Publishing, 1920.

Hewitt, Foster. *Hockey Night in Canada*. Toronto: Ryerson Press, 1958.

Hoffman, Arnold. *Free Gold: The Story of Canadian Mining*. New York and Toronto: Rinehart and Company, 1947.

Jenkinson, Sir Anthony. *Where Seldom a Gun Is Heard*. London: Arthur Baker, 1937.

LeBourdais, D.M. *Metals and Men: The Story of Canadian Mining*. Toronto: McClelland & Stewart, 1957.

Logan, Anne M. *From Tent to Tower: The Biography of Sydney H. Logan*. Toronto: self-published, 1974.

McCollum, Watt Hugh. *Who Owns Canada?: An Examination of the Facts Concerning the Concentration of Ownership and Control of the Means of Production, Distribution and Exchange in Canada*. Ottawa: Woodsworth House Publishers, 1947.

Moore, William Henry. *Yellow Metal*. Toronto: Printers Guild, 1934.

Selke, Frank J., with Gordon Green. *Behind the Cheering*. Toronto: McClelland & Stewart, 1962.

Smythe, Conn, with Scott Young. *If You Can't Beat 'em in the Alley*. Toronto: McClelland & Stewart, 1981.

Trigge, Arthur St. L. *A History of The Canadian Bank of Commerce, with an account of the other banks which now form part of its organization,* vol. 3: 1919–1930. Toronto: The Canadian Bank of Commerce, 1934.

Letters, Fonds, Personal Memoirs

The Beaverbrook Papers, Parliamentary Archives, London, England

T. Eaton Co. Fond, Archives of Ontario

Hepburn Papers

The John Paris Bickell Bequest, Art Gallery of Ontario

John Paris Bickell Family Files, courtesy of Graham MacLachlan

Lord Beaverbrook Fonds, Beaverbrook Library, London, England

McIntyre Research Foundation Fonds, Archives of Ontario

Ross and Macdonald Archive, Canadian Centre for Architecture

Conn Smythe Fonds, Archives of Ontario

Theatre Plans, Archives of Ontario

Various materials, City of Toronto Archives

Various materials, Hockey Hall of Fame Resource Centre

Various materials, Toronto Reference Library

Periodicals

Andrean

Billboard

Caduceus

Canadian Journal of Film Studies

Canadian Medical Association Journal

Citizen-Advertiser (Auburn, NY)

Collier's

Construction: A Journal for the Architectural Engineering and Contracting Interest of Canada

Dorchester Review

Evening Independent (St. Petersburg, FL)

Evening Telegram (New York, NY)

The Film Daily

Financial Post

Flight

Fort Pierce News Tribune (Fort Pierce, FL)

Globe

Globe and Mail

Huron Expositor

Hush

International Journal of the History of Sport

Journal of the Royal Architectural Institute of Canada

Journal of the Society for the Study of Architecture in Canada

Lethbridge Herald

Maple Leaf (Annual)

Miami News

Mississauga News

Moving Picture World

New York Clipper

New York Post

New York Times

Northern Miner (Cobalt/Toronto)

Ottawa Citizen

Ottawa Journal

Porcupine Advance

The Review (St. Andrew's College)

Sandusky Register

Sarasota Herald-Tribune

Saturday Evening Post

Saturday Night

Spirit of Schumacher

Sporting Life
Star Weekly (Toronto)
Timmins Daily Press
Toronto Daily News
Toronto Daily Star
Toronto Mail and Empire
Toronto Star
Toronto Sun
Toronto Telegram
Toronto World
Utica Observer Dispatch
Winnipeg Free Press
Winnipeg Tribune

Articles, Court Documents, Government Documents, Interviews, and Miscellaneous

Art Gallery of Ontario. "Catalogue: John Paris Bickell." Toronto: Art Gallery of Ontario.

Arthur, E.R. "The Toronto Chapter Architectural Exhibition," *Journal of the Royal Architectural Institute of Canada*, 6 March 1929.

Barthelmes *v.* Bickell, 1921 62 S.C.R. 599. Supreme Court of Canada, 9 December 1921.

Bickell, John Paris. "Last Will and Testament of John Paris Bickell." Toronto: 2 February 1951.

——. "President's Address to Sports Followers of the Queen City," *Maple Leaf Gardens Official Programme*, Toronto Maple Leafs *v.* Chicago Black Hawks. Toronto: 12 November 1931.

The Canadian Bank of Commerce. *Annual Report*. Toronto: The Canadian Bank of Commerce, 1951.

Clarke, James Paton. "Lays of the Maple Leaf," Songs of Canada. Toronto: A.S. Nordheimer, c.1853 (sheet music/poetry).

Construction: A Journal for the Architectural Engineering and Contracting Interests of Canada 19.10 (Toronto: October 1926).

Correspondence with Jennifer Rieger, manager of the Grange House. Toronto: January–February 2013.

Current Account, Staff Magazine of the Canadian Bank of Commerce. Toronto: The Canadian Bank of Commerce (September 1951).

Davis, Forrest. "Sell 'Em Ben Smith: The Epic of a Rover Boy in Wall Street," *Saturday Evening Post*, 211.32 (4 February 1939).

Interview with Anne M. Logan. 26 June 2014.

Interview with John K. Cooke. 8 February 2014.

J.P. Bickell & Co. *v.* Cutten, 1925 19. Ontario Court of Appeals, 6 April 1925.

Lee *v.* Bickell, 292 U.S. 415, United States Supreme Court, 21 May 1934.

Maloof *v.* Bickell and Company, 59 S.C.R. 429. Supreme Court of Canada, 22 December 1919.

Maple Leaf Gardens Limited. "Manuscript," placed in the cornerstone of the Maple Leaf Gardens. Toronto: 21 September 1931.

McPhail, I.A., F.C. Biggar, and R.K. McCarthy, eds. "Ourselves," *The Caduceus*, Staff Magazine of the Canadian Bank of Commerce 22.1 (Toronto: The Canadian Bank of Commerce, January 1941).

Mississaugua Golf and Country Club. "By-Law Number 57," Official Records of the Mississaugua Golf and Country Club Limited. Mississauga: 19 April 1937.

Mitcham, Paul A. "Proposed Heritage Designation Bickell Estate, 1993, 2009 and 2025 Mississauga Road (Ward 8)," *Corporate Report*. Mississauga: 20 July 2007.

National Trust Company Limited. "Minutes." Toronto: National Trust Company Limited, 5 September 1951.

Official Hockey Program, Arena Gardens, Fonds 70, Series 306, Subseries 1, File 23, City of Toronto Archives. November 1930.

Ontario Department of Mines. *Annual Report*, 45.1 (1936). Toronto: T.E. Bowman, 1937.

Royal Canadian Yacht Club. *By-Laws: Regulations and List of Members of the Royal Canadian Yacht Club*. May 1911.

Taylor, Reid. "Only a Free Market for Gold Will Save the Nation," Congressional Record — Senate 14533. Washington: 16 August 1954.

Toronto City Directories. 1906, 1908, 1913, and 1920.

Secondary Sources

Books

Barnes, Michael. *Fortunes in the Ground: Cobalt, Porcupine and Kirkland Lake*. Toronto and Erin, ON: Stoddart Publishing and The Boston Mills Press (1986) 1993.

——. *Timmins: The Porcupine Country*. Erin, ON: The Boston Mills Press, 1991.

Bennett, Tony. *The Birth of the Museum: History, Theory, Politics*. London: Routledge, 1995.

Conrad, Margaret, and Alvin Finkel. *History of the Canadian Peoples: 1867 to the Present*, vol. 2, 4th ed. Toronto: Pearson Longman, 2006.

Cosentino, Frank. *The Renfrew Millionaires: The Valley Boys of Winter 1910*. Burnstown, ON: General Store Publishing House, 1990.

Diamond, Dan, et al. *Total Hockey: The Official Encyclopaedia of the National Hockey League*, 2nd ed. New York: Total Sports Publishing, 2000.

Dow, James. *The Arrow: The Dramatic Story of a Pioneering Canadian Aircraft Maker and Its Legendary Supersonic Fighter*. Toronto: James Lorimer & Company, 1997.

Fancy, Peter. *Temiskaming Treasure Trails: 1916–1922*. Cobalt, ON: Highway Book Shop, 1994.

Fong, William. *J.W. McConnell: Financier, Philanthropist, Patriot.* Montreal and Kingston: McGill-Queen's UP, 2008.

Francis, R. Douglas, Richard Jones, and Donald B. Smith. *Destinies: Canadian History Since Confederation,* 6th ed. Toronto: Nelson Education, 2008.

Galland, Adolf. *The First and the Last: Germany's Fighter Force in WWII,* Fortunes of War Series. Black Hawk, CO: Cerberus Press, 2005.

Grant, Alexander. *Independence and Nationhood: Scotland 1306–1469.* Edinburgh: Edinburgh UP, 1984.

Gruneau, Richard, and David Whitson. *Hockey Night in Canada: Sport, Identities and Cultural Politics.* Toronto: Garamond Press, 1993.

Hall, John E., Evelyne Cassan, and Bettie Bradley. *Mississauga Golf and Country Club: 1906–1981,* 75th Anniversary Book. Mississauga: Mississaugua Golf and Country Club, Limited, 1981.

Hewitt, Foster. *Foster Hewitt: His Own Story.* Toronto: The Ryerson Press, 1967.

Holzman, Morey, and Joseph Niefort. *Deceptions and Doublecross: How the NHL Conquered Hockey.* Toronto: Dundurn Press, 2002.

Houston, William. *Inside Maple Leaf Gardens: The Rise and Fall of the Toronto Maple Leafs.* Toronto: McGraw Hill-Ryerson, 1989.

Iveson, Tony, and Brad Milton. *Lancaster: The Biography.* London: Andre Deutsch, 2009.

Kinnane, Adrian. *Jack Kent Cooke: A Career Biography.* Lansdowne, VA: Jack Kent Cooke Foundation, 2004.

Lemon, James. *Toronto Since 1918.* Toronto: James Lorimer, 1985.

McParland, Kelly. *The Lives of Conn Smythe: From the Battlefield to Maple Leaf Gardens.* Toronto: Fenn / McClelland & Stewart, 2012.

Middlebrook, Martin. *The Battle of Hamburg: The Firestorm Raid.* London: Cassell Military Paperbacks (1980), 2000.

Miller, Ian Hugh MacLean. *Our Glory and Our Grief: Torontonians and the Great War*. Toronto: U of Toronto P, 2002.

Myers, Jay. *The Fitzhenry and Whiteside Book of Canadian Facts and Dates*, revised and updated by Larry Hoffman and Fraser Sutherland. Richmond Hill: Fitzhenry and Whiteside, 1991.

Norrie, Kenneth, and Douglas Owram. *A History of the Canadian Economy*. Toronto: Harcourt Brace Jovanovich Canada, 1991.

Rudy, Jarrett. *The Freedom to Smoke*. Montreal and Kingston: McGill-Queen's UP, 2005.

Rumilly, Robert. *Histoire de la Société Saint-Jean-Baptiste de Montréal: des patriotes au Fleurdelisé, 1834–1948*. Collection connaissance des pays québécois, 13. Montreal: L'Aurore, 1975.

Saywell, John T. *"Just call me Mitch": The Life of Mitchell F. Hepburn*. Toronto: U of Toronto P, 1991.

Seiler, Robert M., and Tamara P. Seiler. *Reel Time: Movie Exhibitors and Movie Audiences in Prairie Canada, 1896 to 1986*. Edmonton: Alberta U Press, 2013.

Shea, Kevin. *Barilko: Without a Trace*. Toronto: Fenn, 2004.

Smith, Philip. *Harvest from the Rock: A History of Mining in Ontario*. Toronto: Macmillan of Canada, 1986.

Staudohar, Paul, and James A. Mangan, eds. *The Business of Professional Sports*. Urbana: U of Illinois P, 1991.

Walden, Keith. *Becoming Modern in Toronto: The Industrial Exhibition and the Shaping of a Late Victorian Culture*. Toronto: U of Toronto P, 1997.

White, Peter. *Investigation into an Alleged Combine in the Motion Picture Industry in Canada*. Ottawa: King's Printer, 1931.

Wilson, Jason. *Soldiers of Song: The Dumbells and Other Canadian Concert Parties of the First World War*. Waterloo: Wilfrid Laurier UP, 2012.

Journal Articles, Chapters, Miscellaneous

Aerial Visuals: Airplane Dossier, official website of Aerial Visuals. www.aerialvisuals.ca.

Air Canada Family, official website of the Air Canada Family. www.acfamily.net.

Barnes, Michael. "Roy Thomson's Timmins Adventures," *Republic of Mining*, 16 June 2008. www.republicofmining.com.

Camp Bickell, official website of Camp Bickell. www.campbickell.com.

Canadian Heritage, Government of Canada. www.pch.gc.ca.

Coffman, Peter. "Casa Loma and the Gothic Imagination," *Journal of the Society for the Study of Architecture in Canada* 3.4 (2003).

Cook, George L., with Marjorie Robinson. "'The Fight of My Life': Alfred Fitzpatrick and Frontier College's Extramural Degree for Working People," *Histoire sociale / Social History* 23.45 (May 1990).

Cowan, Paul. "Canadians in Defence of the Raj, 1858," *Dorchester Review* 3.2 (Autumn/Winter 2013).

The Dam Busters, directed by Michael Anderson. UK: Association British Pathé, 1955 (film).

Field, Russell. "'There's more people here tonight than at a first night of the Metropolitan': Professional Hockey Spectatorship in the 1920s and 1930s in New York and Toronto," in Andrew Holman, ed. *Canada's Game: Hockey and Identity*, Montreal and Kingston: McGill-Queen's UP, 2009.

——. "Constructing the Preferred Spectator: Arena Design and Operation and the Consumption of Hockey in 1930s Toronto," *International Journal of the History of Sport* 25.6 (May 2008).

Filey, Mike. "Canada Zoomed Ahead with Ambitious Jetliner," *Toronto Sketches: "The Way We Were."* Toronto and Oxford: Dundurn Press, 1992.

George Weston Limited, official website. www.weston.ca.

Hannaford Street Silver Band, Howard Cable, *Northern Delights*. Burlington, ON: Opening Day Recordings 1996 (audio/CD).

Heritage Planning, official website. www.mississauga.ca.

J.P. Bickell Foundation. "A Four-Year Report to August 2011," 27. Toronto: J.P. Bickell Foundation, 2011.

Legends of Hockey, official website of the Hockey Hall of Fame. www.legendsofhockey.net.

The Longines Symphonette Society, *Hockey Night in Canada*. Toronto: HNIC 1, c. 1971 (audio/LP).

Mills, David. "The Blue Line and the Bottom Line: Entrepreneurs and the Business of Hockey in Canada, 1927–1990," in Paul Staudohar and James A. Mangan, eds., *The Business of Professional Sports*. Urbana: U of Illinois P, 1991.

The Mining Hall of Fame, official website. www.mininghalloffame.ca.

Moore, Paul S. "Nathan L. Nathanson Introduces Canadian Odeon: Producing National Competition in Film Exhibition," *Canadian Journal of Film Studies* 12.2 (Fall 2003).

Muir, Alexander. "The Maple Leaf Forever," A Canadian National Song, words and music by Alexander Muir. Toronto: self-published, 1867 (sheet music).

Rice, Gitz. "Take Me Back to the Land of Promise." Montreal: Berliner, His Master's Voice, no. 216016, 1917 (audio/78 rpm).

SickKids Foundation, official website of SickKids Foundation. www.sickkidsfoundation.com.

Théâtre St-Denis, official website. www.theatrestdenis.com.

Image Credits

American Aviation Magazine: 153
Anne Logan Collection: 111, 112
City of Toronto Archives: 97 (Fonds 1257, Series 1057, Item 2800)
Construction Magazine: 120, 124
Imperial Oil / Turofsky Collection, Hockey Hall of Fame: 102, 181
Joe Campbell Collection: 177
MacLachlan Family Collection: 17, 20, 23, 24, 29, 30, 33, 34, 38, 40, 43, 44, 46, 48, 56, 57, 61, 62 (top and bottom), 65, 67, 95, 103 (all), 105 (top), 108, 109, 116, 121, 122, 128, 129, 130, 135, 136, 143, 144, 151 (all), 154 (all), 155, 183, 184, 185, 186
Maple Leaf Gardens Limited: 93, 94
Michael Davidson Collection: 179
Michael Martchenko Collection: 142
Motor Boating Magazine: 52, 55 (all)
RM Sothesby's: 47 (top)
Scotiabank: 105 (bottom)
St. Andrew's Presbyterian Church: 22
Toronto Telegram Collection: 89

Index

Page numbers in italics indicate images and captions.